The Fyddeye Guide to
America's Veteran Warships

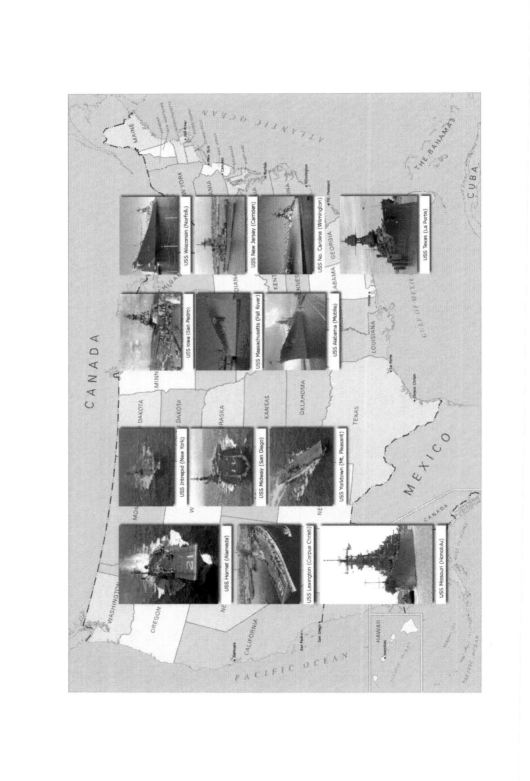

The Fyddeye Guide to America's Veteran Warships

500+ Historic Warships, Tugboats, Cargo Ships, and Tall Ships You Can Visit Today

Edited by Joe Follansbee

With a foreword by maritime archaeologist and

curator Nathaniel Howe

Hello Steven,
Cdy Eals told me he thought of you,
when he saw my book. Enjoy!
Joe Follansbee

To all the men and women fighting to preserve our maritime heritage

CONTENTS

INTRODUCTION

Welcome to *The Fyddeye Guide to Veteran Warships*, your guide to America's most important historic warships, as well as tugboats, Coast Guard vessels, commercial vessels, and tall ships. As a continent-spanning nation bounded on the east and west by vast oceans, America is defined by the sea. The earliest Anglo-European colonists took huge risks when they set sail across the Atlantic Ocean for New England or journeyed around Cape Horn to start new lives in what they'd later call California. Many looked fondly back at the ships that were their temporary homes for many months.

As the country developed, vessels of all sizes expressed the nation's personality and aspirations. Powerful aircraft carriers, battleships, and destroyers projected political power to all corners of the globe. Cargo carriers generated wealth for the owners, jobs for the mariners, and, in many cases, comfortable lives for their families. Other kinds of vessels, workhorses such as ferries and tugboats, assisted these ventures. Today, the country's collection of tall ships preserve the skills and culture that made these journeys possible.

Most ships and boats have a relatively short life, maybe 20 or 30 years, if they're cared for. But some are so important that their owners or former sailors want to preserve them as a way to remember a former way of life or a memorial to a great endeavor. One of the best examples is the USS Missouri, the battleship that witnessed the surrender of Imperial Japan on September 2, 1945, signaling the end of World War II. The ship is now in Honolulu, Hawaii, welcoming children, veterans and tourists, her guns forever silent. *The Fyddeye Guide to America's Veteran Warships* lists nearly 250 of these preserved military vessels, and an almost equal number of non-military boats and ships, most of which you can visit. They range from huge warcraft to small craft you might miss in a marina if you didn't know they were there. Many are maintained by military or civilian veterans who sailed in them, or their descendants. All are important to America's story.

The Fyddeye Guide to Veteran Warships is the most comprehensive list of historic vessels in print, but it's by no means perfect. I started my research by reviewing the first book in the series, *The Fyddeye Guide to America's Maritime History*, published in 2010. I sadly discovered that a handful of vessels had been lost, sold for scrap, or in a few cases, vanished from the record. By the same token, I found a few small craft that I had either missed or had graduated from ordinary working boats to the status of historical artifact. Most of the higher-profile vessels have an associated website, from which I pulled certain items, such as a phone number. Some have Facebook, Twitter or Instagram accounts. However, data such as email address or hours of operation can change without notice, and the website is sometimes the last place that's updated.

If you decide to visit an historic ship or its associated museum, always contact the organization first to confirm hours, admission prices, and any access restrictions.

I've set up the *Fyddeye Guide to America's Veteran Warships* to make it as easy as possible to find and visit a historic vessel. Most are owned and operated by non-profit historical societies or small museums. Ninety percent or more of these organizations are supported by a small, but dedicated cadre of volunteers and donors who are the unsung heroes of maritime heritage preservation and interpretation.

A government or foundation may award a grant now and then, but the hard work, including fundraising, is accomplished by local citizens proud of their community's history and landmarks. Respect their work, and put a few dollars in the donation jar when you visit. Better yet, become a member of your own local history society or community museum. You'll be amazed at what you'll discover about your home town and its history.

– Joe Follansbee, May, 2021

How to read a listing in the *Fyddeye Guide to America's Veteran Warships*.

HORNET

Launched in 1943, the World War II-era aircraft carrier USS Hornet also played a role in the Apollo space program in the 1960s. It is now a museum ship. *Address:* 707 W Hornet Ave., Pier 3 *City:* Alameda *State:* CA *Zip:* 94501 *Phone:* 510-521-8448 *Web:* www.uss-hornet.org *Email:* info@uss-hornet.org *Visitors welcome?* Yes *Hours:* Saturday and Sunday, 10 a.m. to 5 p.m. *Admission:* $20 adults; $15 seniors, students, military; $10 youth six to 17; under six FREE *Operated by:* Aircraft Carrier Hornet Foundation **NR? Yes NHL? Yes** *Built:* 1943 *Latitude:* 37.7721 *Longitude:* -122.2960

- *Address/City/State/Zip:* Street address or approximate location. Note that some ships, such as excursion vessels, move around; They may be temporarily away from their berths.
- *Phone:* Information phone
- *Web:* Website. Links to social media pages are often found on the home page.
- *Email:* Email address
- *Visitors welcome?* Available for tours or visits? (Yes/No)
- *Hours:* Operating hours, if available for visits
- *Admission:* Admission fee, if available for visits
- *Operated by:* Organization operating the attraction
- *NR?* Is the attraction listed on the National Register of Historic Places?
- *NHL?* Is the attraction listed as a National Historic Landmark?
- *Built:* Year launched
- *Latitude/Longitude:* Approximate geo-location of the attraction

Note: The National Register of Historic Places is the sofficial list of cultural resources worthy of preservation in the United States. If the attraction is on the Register, this item is **bolded.** A National Historic Landmark is on a similar list, but more prestigious and exclusive with tighter criteria. If the attraction is a Landmark, this item is **bolded.** The latitude and longitude items are based on information, such as addresses, provided by the attraction owner or listed in publicly accessible map resources. Readers should double-check these before using them in GPS-enabled devices.

Are you on Facebook, Twitter, or Instagram? Check the listed websites to find links to a ship's social media accounts.

FOREWORD

Museum ships and their care, preservation, and interpretation is not simply my profession, but a lifelong passion grown from my own childhood museum ship experiences and an early fascination with maritime history. By age twelve, Saturday morning cartoons were displaced by *Moby-Dick*, Pearl Harbor, and the Battle of the Atlantic. A favorite among my maritime-themed VHS tapes was the 1952 television series, *Victory at Sea*, a 26-part saga chronicling the naval campaigns of World War II. Soon, I was frenetically building ship models and begging my parents to turn every family trip into a maritime museum tour, visiting sailing ships like the whaler Charles W. Morgan or the battleship USS Missouri.

On board these surviving museum ships, the black-and-white film footage I so eagerly absorbed came alive; the smells of tar, paint, and engine oil, the hum of ventilation fans, and the feel of heavy armor plate growing hot in the sun. It is an awesome feeling to stand on a bridge wing where momentous historical events happened, to see where the Imperial Japanese surrender was signed on the deck of the USS Missouri, meet docents who sailed on the ship as young men, or to see the cargo hold of a great square-rigger where the economic lifeblood of a region was stowed for an ocean passage.

There is an incredible power in museum ships, a tangible connection with history, transporting us to other times, places, and hardships. They are macro-artifacts, so large that you can go aboard and have a truly immersive experience, completely enveloped in the artifact you are visiting. Built as mobile and self-contained worlds, fortified against the elements, and able to travel to historic events rather than wait for them to pass through, they are unlike any other artifact or historic site.

My most moving museum ship experience was aboard the World War II Liberty Ship, Jeremiah O'Brien. As we were steaming out of San Francisco Bay, as was so often shown in *Victory at Sea*, I gazed up at the Golden Gate Bridge and, for a moment, felt I was in my grandfather's shoes. He must've looked up at that bridge from the deck of his troopship as he departed on his fifteen wartime voyages to the South Pacific as a Navy surgeon. Jeremiah O'Brien, one of the lucky few museum ships in operational condition, welded my connection to my grandfather in a very special way, years after he had passed. I doubt any other kind of artifact or mode of historic interpretation could have done that as powerfully and poignantly as that veteran cargo ship steaming into the Pacific swell.

This book is a framework for you to find and visit America's incredibly diverse national collection of museum ships, both naval and civilian. I have also come to learn that most civilian vessels have war stories to tell too. Museum vessels provide clear and tangible windows into our national, economic, technological, and social history, and often our own personal histories as well.

Nathaniel Howe, Seattle, 2021

Nathaniel Howe is a nautical archaeologist, maritime historian, and former executive director of Northwest Seaport Maritime Heritage Center in Seattle. He's worked on the historic vessels S/V Wawona (1897), M/V Arthur Foss (1889), LV-83 Swiftsure (1904), and F/V Tordenskjold (1911). He's also former curator of the four-masted bark Pommern (1903) at the Åland Maritime Museum in Mariehamn, Finland.

1

WARSHIPS: WORLD WAR II

The USS Missouri is a military memorial at Pearl Harbor in Honolulu, Hawaii. (Photo: Wikimedia Commons)

Veterans' groups, museums, and historical societies have preserved more ships from the World War II era than any other conflict. The vessels range from aircraft carriers to PT boats. Many, usually the smaller craft, are maintained in operating condition.

Aircraft Carriers

HORNET

Launched in 1943, the World War II-era aircraft carrier USS Hornet also played a role in the Apollo space program in the 1960s. It is now a museum ship. *Address:* 707 W Hornet Ave., Pier 3 *City:* Alameda *State:* CA *Zip:* 94501 *Phone:* 510-521-8448 *Web:* www.uss-hornet.org *Email:* info@uss-hornet.org *Visitors welcome?* Yes *Hours:* Saturday and Sunday, 10 a.m. to 5 p.m. *Admission:* $20 adults; $15 seniors, students, military; $10 youth six to 17; under six FREE *Operated by:* Aircraft Carrier Hornet Foundation **NR? Yes NHL? Yes** *Built:* 1943 *Latitude:* 37.7721 *Longitude:* -122.2960

INTREPID

Launched in 1943, the World War II-era aircraft carrier USS Intrepid is the premier exhibit of the Intrepid Sea, Air & Space Museum. *Address:* Pier 86, W. 46th St. and 12th Ave. *City:* New York *State:* NY *Zip:* 05933 *Phone:* 212-245-0072 Toll-free: 877-957-7447 *Web:* www.intrepidmuseum.org *Visitors welcome?* Yes *Hours:* Thursday to Sunday, 10 a.m. to 5 p.m. *Admission:* $33 adults; $31 seniors; $24 youth five to 12; under five FREE *Operated by:* Intrepid Sea-Air-Space Museum **NR? Yes NHL? Yes** *Built:* 1943 *Latitude:* 40.7631 *Longitude:* -73.9996

LEXINGTON

Launched in 1942, the World War II-era aircraft carrier USS Lexington is now a floating exhibit and museum ship. *Address:* 2914 N. Shoreline Blvd. *City:* Corpus Christi *State:* TX *Zip:* 23076 *Phone:* 361-888-4873 *Web:* www.usslexington.com *Email:* rocco@usslexington.com *Visitors welcome?* Yes *Hours:* Labor Day to Memorial Day, 9 a.m. to 6 p.m.; Memorial Day to Labor Day and Spring Break, 9 a.m. to 5 p.m. *Admission:* $18.95 adults, $16.95 seniors, youth 13-17, $14.95 active military; $13.95 children four to 12; under four FREE *Operated by:* USS Lexington Museum on the Bay *NR?* No **NHL? Yes** *Built:* 1942 *Latitude:* 27.8149 *Longitude:* -97.3889

MIDWAY

Launched in 1945 just as World War II ended, the aircraft carrier USS Midway is the centerpiece of the USS Midway Museum. *Address:* 910 N. Harbor Dr. *City:* San Diego *State:* CA *Zip:* 92101 *Phone:* 619-544-9600 *Web:* www.midway.org *Visitors welcome?* Yes *Hours:* Daily, 10 a.m. to 4 p.m. *Admission:* $26 adults; $18 seniors, students, veterans; children six and under FREE *Operated by:* USS Midway Museum *NR?* No *NHL?* No *Built:* 1945 *Latitude:* 32.7147 *Longitude:* -117.1740

YORKTOWN

Launched in 1943, the World War II-era aircraft carrier USS Yorktown is the centerpiece of the Patriots Point Naval & Maritime Museum. *Address:* 40 Patriots Point Road *City:* Mount Pleasant *State:* SC *Zip:* 29464 *Phone:* 843-884-2727 Toll-free: 866-831-1720 *Web:* www.patriotspoint.org *Visitors welcome?* Yes *Hours:* Daily, 9:30 a.m. to 6 p.m. *Admission:* $27 adults, $19 seniors, $16 children six to 11, under six FREE *Operated by:* Patriots Point Naval & Maritime Museum **NR? Yes NHL? Yes** *Built:* 1943 *Latitude:* 32.7940 *Longitude:* -79.9051

Battleships

ALABAMA

Launched in 1942, the battleship USS Alabama is now a floating exhibit and museum ship. *Address:* 2703 Battleship Parkway *City:* Mobile *State:* AL *Zip:* 36601 *Phone:* 251-433-2703 *Web:* www.ussalabama.com *Email:* info@ussalabama.com *Visitors welcome?* Yes *Hours:* October to March, daily, 8 a.m. to 4 p.m.; April to Sept., daily, 8 a.m. to 6 p.m. *Admission:* $15 adults, $13 seniors, $6 children six to 11, under six FREE *Operated by:* Battleship Memorial Park **NR? Yes** *NHL?* No *Latitude:* 30.6818 *Longitude:* -88.0148

IOWA

Launched in 1943, the World War II-era battleship USS Iowa is a museum ship on the San Pedro, Calif., waterfront. *Address:* 250 S. Harbor Blvd. *City:* San Pedro *State:* CA *Zip:* 90731 *Phone:* 310-971-4462 *Web:* www.pacificbattleship.com *Visitors welcome?* Yes *Hours:* Daily, 10 a.m. to 4 p.m. *Admission:* $22.95 adults *Operated by:* Battleship Iowa Museum *NR?* No *NHL?* No *Built:* 1943 *Latitude:* 33.7422 *Longitude:* -118.2773

MASSACHUSETTS

Launched in 1942, the World War II-era battleship USS Massachusetts is a floating exhibit and memorial at Battleship Cove. *Address:* 5 Water St. *City:* Fall River *State:* MA *Zip:* 02722 *Phone:* 508-678-1100 *Web:* www.battleshipcove.org *Email:*

battleship@battleshipcove.org *Visitors welcome?* Yes *Hours:* Daily, 9 a.m. to 5 p.m. *Admission:* $25 adults, $23 seniors, $16 active military, $15 children four to 12, children three and under FREE *Operated by:* Battleship Cove *NR? Yes NHL? Yes Built:* 1942 *Latitude:* 41.7040 *Longitude:* -71.1597

MISSOURI

Launched in 1944, the battleship USS Missouri was the site where the Imperial Japanese surrendered at the end of World War II. *Address:* 1 Arizona Memorial Road *City:* Honolulu *State:* HI *Zip:* 96818 *Phone:* 808-455-1600 *Web:* www.ussmissouri.org *Visitors welcome?* Yes *Hours:* Tuesday to Saturday, 8 a.m. to 4 p.m. *Admission:* $22.99 adults, $13.99 children four to 12 *Operated by:* USS Missouri Memorial Association *NR? Yes NHL?* No *Built:* 1944 *Latitude:* 21.3643 *Longitude:* -157.9370

NEW JERSEY

Launched in 1943, the World War II-era battleship New Jersey is a now a floating museum. *Address:* 100 Clinton Street *City:* Camden *State:* NJ *Zip:* 08103 *Phone:* 856-966-1652 *Web:* www.battleshipnewjersey.org *Email:* info@battleshipnewjersey.org *Visitors welcome?* Yes *Hours:* Daily, 11 a.m. to 3 p.m. *Admission:* Contact attraction directly *Operated by:* Battleship New Jersey Museum and Memorial *NR?* No *NHL?* No *Built:* 1943 *Latitude:* 39.9347 *Longitude:* -75.1108

NORTH CAROLINA

Launched in 1941, the World War II-era battleship North Carolina is now a museum and war memorial. *Address:* One Battleship Road *City:* Wilmington *State:* NC *Zip:* 28402 *Phone:* 910-251-5797 *Web:* www.battleshipnc.com *Email:* exdir@battleshipnc.com *Visitors welcome?* Yes *Hours:* Daily, 8 a.m. to 5 p.m. *Admission:* $14 adults, $10 seniors, military, $6 children six to 11, children five and under FREE *Operated by:* Battleship North Carolina *NR? Yes NHL? Yes Built:* 1941 *Latitude:* 34.2349 *Longitude:* -77.9533

WISCONSIN

The USS Wisconsin is an Iowa-class battleship that served in World War II, the Korean War, and the First Gulf War after a period of deactivation. She is now a museum ship at Nauticus in Norfolk, Virginia. *Address:* One Waterside Drive *City:* Norfolk *State:* VA *Zip:* 23510 *Phone:* 757-664-1000 *Web:* nauticus.org *Visitors welcome?* Yes *Hours:* Wednesday to Saturday, 10 a.m. – 5 p.m.; Sunday, Noon to 5 p.m. *Admission:* $15.95 adults, $11.50 children *Operated by:* Nauticus **NR? Yes** NHL? No *Built:* 1943 *Latitude:* 36.8442 *Longitude:* -76.2878

Cruisers

FALL RIVER

Launched in 1944, the World War II and Korean War-era cruiser USS Fall River is now a floating exhibit at Battleship Cove. *Address:* 5 Water St. *City:* Fall River *State:* MA *Zip:* 02722 *Phone:* 508-678-1100 Toll-free: 800-533-3194 *Web:* www.battleshipcove.org *Email:* battleship@battleshipcove.org *Visitors welcome?* Yes *Hours:* Daily, 9 a.m. to 5 p.m. *Admission:* $25 adults, $23 seniors, $16 active military, $15 children four to 12, children three and under FREE *Operated by:* Battleship Cove *NR?* No *NHL?* No *Built:* 1944 *Latitude:* 41.7040 *Longitude:* -71.1597

LITTLE ROCK

Launched in 1945, the cruiser USS Little Rock, first a World War II-era cruiser and later refitted with guided missiles, is a floating exhibit on the Buffalo waterfront. *Address:* One Naval Park Cove *City:* Buffalo *State:* NY *Zip:* 14202 *Phone:* 716-847-1773 *Web:* www.buffalonavalpark.org *Email:* info@buffalonavalpark.org *Visitors welcome?* Yes *Hours:* Wednesday to Sunday, 10 a.m. to 5 p.m. *Admission:* $16 adults, $13 seniors, $12 veteran, $10 children five to 12, children under four FREE *Operated by:* Buffalo and Erie County Naval & Military Park *NR?* No *NHL?* No *Built:* 1945 *Latitude:* 42.8994 *Longitude:* -78.8759

Destroyers

CASSIN YOUNG

USS Cassin Young was built by Bethlehem Steel Corporation at San Pedro, California and commissioned on December 31, 1943. *Address:*

Boston National Historic Park, Charlestown Navy Yard *City:* Boston *State:* MA *Zip:* 02129 *Phone:* 617-242-5601 *Web:* www.nps.gov/bost/historyculture/usscassinyoung.htm *Visitors welcome?* Yes *Hours:* Daily, 9 a.m. to 5 p.m. *Admission:* FREE *Operated by:* National Park Service *NR?* No *NHL?* No *Built:* 1943 *Latitude:* 42.3722 *Longitude:* -71.0546

JOSEPH P. KENNEDY

Launched in 1945, the World War II-era destroyer USS Joseph P. Kennedy, Jr. is a floating exhibit at Battleship Cove. *Address:* 5 Water St. *City:* Fall River *State:* MA *Zip:* 02722 *Phone:* 508-678-1100 Toll-free: 800-533-3194 *Web:* www.battleshipcove.org *Email:* battleship@battleshipcove.org *Visitors welcome?* Yes *Hours:* Daily, 9 a.m. to 5 p.m. *Admission:* $25 adults, $23 seniors, $16 active military, $15 children four to 12, children three and under FREE *Operated by:* Battleship Cove **NR? Yes NHL? Yes** *Built:* 1945 *Latitude:* 41.7040 *Longitude:* -71.1597

KIDD

Launched in 1943, the World War II-era destroyer USS Kidd is now a floating exhibit and veterans memorial. *Address:* 305 South River Road *City:* Baton Rouge *State:* LA *Zip:* 70802 *Phone:* 225-342-1942 *Web:* www.usskidd.com *Visitors welcome?* Yes *Hours:* Daily, 9:30 a.m. to 3:30 p.m. *Admission:* $12.53 adults, $10.45 seniors, active military, $8.36 children five to 12, under five FREE *Operated by:* USS Kidd Veterans Museum **NR? Yes NHL? Yes** *Built:* 1943 *Latitude:* 30.4444 *Longitude:* -91.1899

LAFFEY

Launched in 1944, the World War II-era destroyer USS Laffey is now a floating exhibit at the Patriots Point Naval & Maritime Museum. *Address:* 40 Patriots Point Road *City:* Mount Pleasant *State:* SC *Zip:* 29464 *Phone:* 843-884-2727 *Web:* www.patriotspoint.org *Visitors welcome?* Yes *Hours:* Daily, 9:30 a.m. to 6 p.m. *Admission:* $27 adults, $19 seniors, $16 children six to 11, under six FREE *Operated by:* Patriots Point Naval & Maritime Museum **NR? Yes NHL? Yes** *Built:* 1944 *Latitude:* 32.7940 *Longitude:* -79.9051

ORLECK

Launched in 1945, the World War II-era destroyer USS Orleck is a floating museum. *Address:* 604 N Enterprise Blvd. *City:* Lake Charles *State:* LA *Phone:* 409-882-9191 *Web:* www.ussorleck.org *Email:* info@ussorleck.org *Visitors welcome?* Yes *Hours:* Monday to Friday, 8 a.m. to 3 p.m., Saturday, 10 a.m. to 4 p.m. *Admission:* $10 adults, $8 seniors, $5 active military, children six to 12, children five and under FREE *Operated by:* Jacksonville Naval Museum *NR?* No *NHL?* No *Built:* 1945

THE SULLIVANS

Launched in 1943, the World War II-era destroyer USS The Sullivans is a floating exhibit on the Buffalo waterfront. *Address:* One Naval Park Cove *City:* Buffalo *State:* NY *Zip:* 14202 *Phone:* 716-847-1773 *Web:* www.buffalonavalpark.org *Email:* info@buffalonavalpark.org *Visitors welcome?* Yes *Hours:* Wednesday to Sunday, 10 a.m. to 5 p.m. *Admission:* $16 adults, $13 seniors, $12 veteran, $10 children five to 12, children under four FREE *Operated by:* Buffalo and Erie County Naval & Military Park ***NR? Yes NHL? Yes*** *Built:* 1943 *Latitude:* 42.8994 *Longitude:* -78.8759

Before visiting any vessel, always call or check the ship's website for changes in hours, admission, or availability.

Destroyer Escorts

SLATER

Launched in 1944, the World War II-era destroyer escort USS Slater is now a floating museum in Albany, New York. *Address:* 141 Broadway *City:* Albany *State:* NY *Zip:* 12202 *Phone:* 518-431-1943 *Web:* www.ussslater.org *Email:* info@ussslater.org *Visitors welcome?* Yes *Hours:* April to November: Wednesday to Sunday, 10 a.m. to 4 p.m. *Admission:* $9 adults, $8 seniors, $7 children six to 14, children five and under FREE *Operated by:* Destroyer Escort Historical Foundation ***NR? Yes*** *NHL?* No *Built:* 1944 *Latitude:* 42.6420 *Longitude:* -73.7510

STEWART

Launched in 1942, the Edsall-class destroyer escort USS Stewart is a dry-berth exhibit at Seawolf Park. *Address:* Seawolf Park, Pelican Island *City:* Galveston *State:* TX *Zip:* 77550 *Phone:* 409-797-5114 *Web:* www.galveston.com/seawolfpark/ *Email:* macm@galvestonparkboard.org *Visitors welcome?* Yes *Hours:* Daily, 8 a.m. to dusk *Admission:* FREE *Operated by:* Seawolf Park *NR?* No *NHL?* No *Built:* 1942 *Latitude:* 29.3316 *Longitude:* -94.8021

Landing Craft

LCI(L)-713

Launched in 1944, the landing craft infantry (large) LCI(L)-713 is a floating museum on the Columbia River. *Address:* 8070 E. Mill Plain Boulevard *City:* Vancouver *State:* WA *Zip:* 98664 *Phone:* 541-226-5427 *Web:* www.amphibiousforces.org *Email:* afmm@amphibiousforces.org *Visitors welcome?* Yes *Hours:* Contact attraction directly *Admission:* Contact attraction directly *Operated by:* Amphibious Forces Memorial Museum *NR?* No *NHL?* No *Built:* 1944 *Latitude:* 45.6254 *Longitude:* -122.5910

LCI(L)-1091

The Humboldt Naval Sea/Air Museum is restoring a World War II-era landing-craft, infantry (large), LCI(L)-1091, as a dry-berth exhibit. *City:* Eureka *State:* CA *Phone:* 707-442-8050 *Visitors welcome?* No *Operated by:* Humboldt Bay Maritime Museum Museum *NR?* No *NHL?* No *Latitude:* 40.8021 *Longitude:* -124.1640

LCM-56

Battleship Cove's artifact collection includes the dry-berthed amphibious LCM 56, one of thousands of short-range craft that delivered men and materiel to invasion beaches, such as Normandy. *Address:* 5 Water St. *City:* Fall River *State:* MA *Zip:* 02722 *Phone:* 508-678-1100 *Web:* www.battleshipcove.org *Visitors welcome?* Yes *Hours:* Daily, 9 a.m. to 5 p.m. *Admission:* $25 adults, $23 seniors, $16 active military, $15 children four to 12, children three and under FREE *Operated by:* Battleship Cove *NR?* No *NHL?* No *Latitude:* 41.7040 *Longitude:* -71.1597

LCS-102

The World War II-era landing craft support ship LCS-102 is now undergoing restoration at Mare Island. *Address:* 289 Waterfront Ave. *City:* Vallejo *State:* CA *Zip:* 94592 *Phone:* 707-373-2159 *Web:* usslcs102.org *Email:* gstutrud@usslcs102.org *Visitors welcome?* Yes *Hours:* Tuesday, Thursday, Saturday, 9 a.m. to 3 p.m. *Admission:* FREE *Operated by:* Landing Craft Support Museum *NR?* No *NHL?* No *Latitude:* 38.0888 *Longitude:* -122.2710

LCT-203

Launched in 1942, the World War II-era landing craft, tank LCT-203, also called Outer Island, is an operating museum vessel. *City:* Bayfield *State:* WI *Phone:* 615-865-0579 *Web:* ww2lct.org *Email:* webmaster@ww2lct.org *Visitors welcome?* Yes *Hours:* Contact attraction directly *Admission:* Contact attraction directly *Operated by:* Outer Island *NR?* No *NHL?* No *Built:* 1942 *Latitude:* 46.8108 *Longitude:* -90.8182

LSM

Launched in 1944, a landing ship, mechanical, LSM, will be part of an exhibit at the Carolina Museum of the Marine in Jacksonville, North Carolina. *Address:* Museum of the Marine *City:* Jacksonville *State:* NC *Zip:* 28541 *Phone:* 910-937-0033 *Web:* www.museumofthemarine.org *Email:* info@museumofthemarine.com *Visitors welcome?* No *Operated by:* Carolina Museum of the Marine *NR?* No *NHL?* No *Built:* 1944 *Latitude:* 34.7538 *Longitude:* -77.4309

LSM-45

Launched in 1944, the medium landing ship LSM-45 is a dry-berth exhibit at Freedom Park in Omaha. *Address:* Freedom Park *City:* Omaha *State:* NE *Phone:* 402-444-7000 *Visitors welcome?* Yes *Hours:* Daily *Admission:* FREE *Operated by:* City of Omaha **NR? Yes NHL? Yes** *Built:* 1944 *Latitude:* 41.2716 *Longitude:* -95.9210

LST-325

Launched in 1943, the landing ship tank LST-325 is now a museum ship. *Address:* 610 NW Riverside Drive *City:* Evansville *State:* IN *Zip:*

47708 *Phone:* 812-435-8678 *Web:* www.lstmemorial.com *Email:* 325office@lstmemorial.org *Visitors welcome?* Yes *Hours:* Tuesday to Sunday, 10 a.m. to 4 p.m. *Admission:* $15 adults, $7.50 children six to 17; under five FREE *Operated by:* USS LST Ship Memorial *NR?* No *NHL?* No *Built:* 1943 *Latitude:* 37.9518 *Longitude:* -87.5760

LST-393

Launched in 1942, the landing ship tank LST 393 is now a floating museum. *Address:* 560 Mart St. *City:* Muskegon *State:* MI *Zip:* 49440 *Phone:* 231-730-1477 *Web:* www.lst393.org *Email:* info@lst393.org *Visitors welcome?* Yes *Hours:* Daily, 10 a.m. to 5 p.m. *Admission:* $10 adults, $5 children five to 17, under four FREE *Operated by:* USS LST 393 Veterans Museum *NR?* No *NHL?* No *Built:* 1942 *Latitude:* 43.2334 *Longitude:* -86.2573

LVCP

The World War II-era landing craft, personnel vehicles (LVCP) is a dry-berth exhibit at the Washington Navy Yard. *Address:* 805 Kidder Breese SE, Washington Navy Yard *City:* Washington *State:* DC *Zip:* 20374 *Phone:* 202-433-6897 *Web:* www.history.navy.mil/ *Visitors welcome?* Yes *Hours:* Monday to Friday, 9 a.m. to 4 p.m., Saturdays, 10 a.m. to 4 p.m. *Admission:* Contact attraction directly *Operated by:* Museum of the United States Navy *NR?* No *NHL?* No *Latitude:* 38.8755 *Longitude:* -76.9935

Liberty & Victory Ships

AMERICAN VICTORY

Launched in 1945, the World War II-era cargo ship American Victory is now a museum vessel. *Address:* 705 Channelside Drive *City:* Tampa *State:* FL *Zip:* 33602 *Phone:* 813-228-8766 *Web:* www.americanvictory.org *Email:* director@americanvictory.org *Visitors welcome?* Yes *Hours:* Monday, noon to 5 p.m., Tuesday to Sunday, 10 a.m. to 5 p.m. *Admission:* $10 adults, $8 seniors/students, $5 veterans, $5 children four to 12, under three FREE *Operated by:* American Victory Museum & Ship *NR?* No *NHL?* No *Built:* 1945 *Latitude:* 27.9440 *Longitude:* -82.4464

JEREMIAH O'BRIEN

Launched in 1943, the World War II-era liberty ship Jeremiah O'Brien is now a museum ship and excursion vessel. *Address:* Pier 45, Fisherman's Wharf *City:* San Francisco *State:* CA *Phone:* 415-544-0100 *Web:* www.ssjeremiahobrien.org *Email:* liberty@ssjeremiahobrien.org *Visitors welcome?* Yes *Hours:* Contact attraction directly *Admission:* Contact attraction directly *Operated by:* National Liberty Ship Memorial, SS Jeremiah O'Brien *NR?* **Yes** *NHL?* **Yes** *Built:* 1943 *Latitude:* 37.8102 *Longitude:* -122.4180

JOHN W. BROWN

Launched in 1942, the World War II-era liberty ship John W. Brown is now a museum ship and excursion vessel. *Address:* Pier 13, 4601 Newgate Ave. *City:* Baltimore *State:* MD *Zip:* 21224 *Phone:* 410-558-0646 *Web:* www.liberty-ship.com *Email:* john.w.brown@usa.net *Visitors welcome?* Yes *Hours:* Contact attraction directly *Admission:* Contact attraction directly *Operated by:* Project Liberty Ship *NR?* **Yes** *NHL?* No *Built:* 1942 *Latitude:* 39.2684 *Longitude:* -76.5688

LANE VICTORY

Launched in 1945, the World War II-era victory ship Lane Victory is now an operational excursion vessel in the Los Angeles area. *Address:* 3011 Miner St. *City:* San Pedro *State:* CA *Zip:* 90731 *Phone:* 310-519-9188 *Web:* www.lanevictory.org *Email:* contact@lanevictory.org *Visitors welcome?* Yes *Hours:* Contact attraction directly *Admission:* $10 adults, $5 children/active military *Operated by:* SS Lane Victory *NR?* **Yes** *NHL?* **Yes** *Built:* 1945 *Latitude:* 33.7172 *Longitude:* -118.2731

RED OAK VICTORY

Launched in 1944, the victory ship Red Oak Victory is a floating exhibit on the Richmond, Calif., waterfront. *Address:* 1337 Canal Blvd., Berth 5 *City:* Richmond *State:* CA *Zip:* 94804 *Phone:* 510-237-2933 *Web:* redoakvictory.us *Email:* info@redoakvictory.us *Visitors welcome?* Yes *Hours:* Sundays, 10 a.m. to 4 p.m. *Admission:* $10 adults *Operated by:* Point Richmond History Association *NR?* **Yes** *NHL?* No *Built:* 1944 *Latitude:* 37.9219 *Longitude:* -122.3500

Minesweepers

HAZARD

Launched in 1944, the World War II-era minesweeper USS Hazard is a dry-berth exhibit at Freedom Park on the Omaha riverfront. *Address:* Freedom Park *City:* Omaha *State:* NE *Phone:* 402-444-7000 *Visitors welcome?* Yes *Hours:* Daily *Admission:* FREE *Operated by:* City of Omaha **NR? Yes NHL? Yes** *Built:* 1944 *Latitude:* 41.2716 *Longitude:* -95.9210

PT Boats & Small Craft

JAPANESE SUICIDE DEMOLITION BOAT

Battleship Cove's artifact collection includes a Japanese suicide demolition boat from World War II. Discovered in a cave and donated to the museum in 1973, the boat has not been positively identified. *Address:* 5 Water St. *City:* Fall River *State:* MA *Zip:* 02722 *Phone:* 508-678-1100 Toll-free: 800-533-3194 *Web:* www.battleshipcove.org *Visitors welcome?* Yes *Hours:* Daily, 9 a.m. to 5 p.m. *Admission:* $25 adults, $23 seniors, $16 active military, $15 children four to 12, children three and under FREE *Operated by:* Battleship Cove *NR?* No *NHL?* No *Latitude:* 41.7040 *Longitude:* -71.1597

P-520

Built in 1944, the P-520 is the last of the 85-foot US Army Air Corps crash boats that rescued downed pilots during WW2 and Korea. *Address:* 2312 S Preston St. *City:* Louisville *State:* KY *Zip:* 40217 *Web:* p520.org *Email:* lewis.palmer@louisvillenavalmuseum.org *Visitors welcome?* No *Hours:* Contact attraction directly *Admission:* Contact attraction directly *Built:* 1944 *Latitude:* 38.2138 *Longitude:* -85.7450

PT-305

The patrol-torpedo boat PT-305 served in European waters during World War II. *Address:* 945 Magazine St. *City:* New Orleans *State:* LA *Zip:* 70130 *Phone:* 504-528-1944 *Web:* www.nationalww2museum.org *Email:* info@nationalww2museum.org *Visitors welcome?* Yes *Hours:* Daily, 9 a.m. to 5 p.m. *Admission:* Contact attraction directly *Operated by:* National World War II Museum *NR?* No *NHL?* No *Latitude:* 29.9430 *Longitude:* -90.0722

PT-309

Launched in 1944, the World War II-era motor torpedo boat PT-309 is a dry-berth exhibit at the National Museum of the Pacific War. *Address:* 340 East Main St. *City:* Fredericksburg *State:* TX *Zip:* 78624 *Phone:* 830-997-8600 *Web:* www.pacificwarmuseum.org *Email:* info@nimitzfoundation.org *Visitors welcome?* Yes *Hours:* Wednesday to Sunday, 11 a.m. to 3 p.m. *Admission:* $18 adults, $14 seniors, $8 students/children six to 17, five and under FREE *Operated by:* Admiral Nimitz Foundation *NR?* No *NHL?* No *Built:* 1944 *Latitude:* 30.2722 *Longitude:* -98.8682

PT-617

Battleship Cove's artifact collection includes PT-617, a small, fast attack boat used primarily in the Pacific theatre of World War II. *Address:* 5 Water St. *City:* Fall River *State:* MA *Zip:* 02722 *Phone:* 508-678-1100 *Web:* www.battleshipcove.org *Visitors welcome?* Yes *Hours:* Daily, 9 a.m. to 5 p.m. *Admission:* $25 adults, $23 seniors, $16 active military, $15 children four to 12, children three and under FREE *Operated by:* Battleship Cove *NR?* No *NHL?* No *Latitude:* 41.7040 *Longitude:* -71.1597

PT 796

Battleship Cove's artifact collection includes PT-796 a small, fast attack boat used primarily in the Pacific theatre of World War II. *Address:* 5 Water St. *City:* Fall River *State:* MA *Zip:* 02722 *Phone:* 508-678-1100 *Web:* www.battleshipcove.org *Visitors welcome?* Yes *Hours:* Daily, 9 a.m. to 5 p.m. *Admission:* $25 adults, $23 seniors, $16 active military, $15 children four to 12, children three and under FREE *Operated by:* Battleship Cove *NR?* No *NHL?* No *Latitude:* 41.7040 *Longitude:* -71.1597

TORPEDO BOAT

The Defenders of America Naval Museum is restoring a World War II-era torpedo boat launched in 1943. *Address:* Defenders of America Museum *City:* Kemah *State:* TX *Phone:* 281-476-0394 *Visitors welcome?*

Yes *Hours:* Contact attraction directly *Admission:* Contact attraction directly *Operated by:* Defenders Of America Naval Museum *NR?* No *NHL?* No *Built:* 1943 *Latitude:* 29.5427 *Longitude:* -95.0205

> Some vessels, especially submarines, limit visitors to four-feet tall or taller for safety reasons. Small children may not be allowed.

Submarines

BATFISH

Launched in 1943, the World War II-ear submarine USS Batfish is a dry-berth exhibit at the USS Batfish War Memorial and Museum. *Address:* Muskogee War Memorial Park *City:* Muskogee *State:* OK *Zip:* 74402 *Phone:* 918-682-6294 *Web:* www.ussbatfish.com *Email:* ussbatfish@sbcglobal.net *Visitors welcome?* Yes *Hours:* Friday and Saturday, 10 a.m. to 6 p.m., Sunday 1 p.m. to 6 p.m. *Admission:* $7 adults, $5 seniors/students/military, $4 children 7-13, children under seven FREE *Operated by:* USS Batfish War Memorial Museum and Park *NR?* No *NHL?* No *Built:* 1943 *Latitude:* 35.7938 *Longitude:* -95.3106

BECUNA

Launched in 1944, the World War II-era Balao-class submarine USS Becuna was decommissioned in 1969 and added to the collection of the Independence Seaport Museum. *Address:* 211 South Columbus Blvd. *City:* Philadelphia *State:* PA *Zip:* 19106 *Phone:* 215-413-8655 *Web:* www.phillyseaport.org *Email:* seaport@phillyseaport.org *Visitors welcome?* Yes *Hours:* Thursday to Saturday, 10 a.m. to 5 p.m., Sunday, noon to 5 p.m. *Admission:* $18 adults; $10 seniors; $14 children, seniors, military; children under two FREE *Operated by:* Independence Seaport Museum ***NR? Yes NHL? Yes*** *Built:* 1944 *Latitude:* 39.9457 *Longitude:* -75.1419

BOWFIN

Launched in 1942, the World War II-era submarine USS Bowfin is a floating exhibit at the Pacific Fleet Submarine Museum. *Address:* 11 Arizona Memorial Drive *City:* Honolulu *State:* HI *Zip:* 96818 *Phone:* 808-423-1341 *Web:* www.bowfin.org *Email:* info@bowfin.org *Visitors welcome?* Yes *Hours:* Daily, 7 a.m. to 5 p.m. *Admission:* $20 adults, $12 children four to 12, under four permitted in museum but not submarine *Operated by:* Pacific Fleet Submarine Memorial Association **NR? Yes NHL? Yes** *Built:* 1942 *Latitude:* 21.3643 *Longitude:* -157.9380

CAVALLA

Launched in 1944, the World War II-era submarine USS Cavalla is a dry-berth display at Seawolf Park on Pelican Island near Galveston. *Address:* Seawolf Park, Pelican Island *City:* Galveston *State:* TX *Zip:* 77550 *Phone:* 409-744-7854 *Web:* www.cavalla.org *Visitors welcome?* Yes *Hours:* Daily, 8 a.m. to dusk *Admission:* FREE *Operated by:* Cavalla Historical Foundation *NR?* No *NHL?* No *Built:* 1944 *Latitude:* 29.3316 *Longitude:* -94.8021

CLAMAGORE

Launched in 1945, the World War II-era submarine USS Clamagore is now a floating exhibit at the Patriots Point Naval & Maritime Museum. *Address:* 40 Patriots Point Road *City:* Mount Pleasant *State:* SC *Zip:* 29464 *Phone:* 843-884-2727 *Web:* www.patriotspoint.org *Visitors welcome?* Yes *Hours:* Daily, 9:30 a.m. to 6 p.m. *Admission:* $27 adults, $19 seniors, $16 children six to 11, under six FREE *Operated by:* Patriots Point Naval & Maritime Museum **NR? Yes NHL? Yes** *Built:* 1945 *Latitude:* 32.7940 *Longitude:* -79.9051

COBIA

Moored along the Manitowoc River, adjacent to the Wisconsin Maritime Museum, is the World War II fleet submarine USS Cobia. Cobia has local and national significance as an icon of Wisconsin's shipbuilding heritage. *Address:* 75 Maritime Drive *City:* Manitowoc *State:* WI *Zip:* 54220 *Phone:* 920-684-0218 *Web:* www.wisconsinmaritime.org *Email:* cgreen@wisconsinmaritime.org *Visitors welcome?* Yes *Hours:* Thursday to Sunday, 10 a.m. to 5 p.m. *Admission:* $15 adults, $12 seniors/veterans, $8 children four to 12, five and under FREE *Operated by:* Wisconsin Maritime Museum *NR?* No *NHL?* No *Built:* 1943 *Latitude:* 44.0931 *Longitude:* -87.6570

COD

Launched in 1943, the World War II-era submarine USS Cod is now a floating exhibit in Cleveland. *Address:* 1089 East 9th Street *City:* Cleveland *State:* OH *Zip:* 44114 *Phone:* 216-408-6991 *Web:* www.usscod.org *Email:* codkeeper@yahoo.com *Visitors welcome?* Yes *Hours:* Contact attraction directly *Admission:* Contact attraction directly *Operated by:* USS Cod Submarine Memorial **NR? Yes NHL? Yes** *Built:* 1943 *Latitude:* 41.5092 *Longitude:* -81.6948

CROAKER

Launched in 1942, the World War II-era submarine USS Croaker is a floating exhibit on the Buffalo waterfront. *Address:* One Naval Park Cove *City:* Buffalo *State:* NY *Zip:* 14202 *Phone:* 716-847-1773 *Web:* www.buffalonavalpark.org *Email:* info@buffalonavalpark.org *Visitors welcome?* Yes *Hours:* Wednesday to Sunday, 10 a.m. to 5 p.m. *Admission:* $16 adults, $13 seniors, $12 veteran, $10 children five to 12, children under four FREE *Operated by:* Buffalo and Erie County Naval & Military Park *NR?* No *NHL?* No *Built:* 1942 *Latitude:* 42.8994 *Longitude:* -78.8759

DRUM

Launched in 1941, the World War II-era submarine USS Drum is now a dry-berth exhibit at Battleship Memorial Park. *Address:* Battleship Memorial Park *City:* Mobile *State:* AL *Zip:* 36601 *Phone:* 251-433-2703 *Web:* www.ussalabama.com *Email:* info@ussalabama.com *Visitors welcome?* Yes *Hours:* October to March, daily, 8 a.m. to 4 p.m.; April to Sept., daily, 8 a.m. to 6 p.m. *Admission:* $15 adults, $13 seniors, $6 children six to 11, under six FREE *Operated by:* USS Alabama Battleship Commission **NR? Yes NHL? Yes** *Built:* 1941 *Latitude:* 30.6818 *Longitude:* -88.0148

HA-8

Launched in 1938, the World War II-era Japanese midget submarine HA-8 is a dry-berth exhibit at the Submarine Force Museum at Naval Base Groton. *Address:* Naval Submarine Base New London *City:* Groton *State:* CT *Zip:* 06349 *Phone:* 860-694-3174 *Web:* www.ussnautilus.org *Email:* info@nautilus.org *Visitors welcome?* Yes *Hours:* May 1 to Sept. 30: Daily, 9 a.m. to 5 p.m.; Winter: Nov. 1 to

April 30, daily, 9 a.m. to 4 p.m. *Admission:* FREE *Operated by:* Naval History & Heritage Command *NR?* No *NHL?* No *Built:* 1938 *Latitude:* 41.3499 *Longitude:* -72.0759

HA-19

Launched in 1938, the Imperial Japanese midget submarine HA-19 is a dry-berth exhibit at the National Museum of the Pacific War. *Address:* 340 East Main St. *City:* Fredericksburg *State:* TX *Zip:* 78624 *Phone:* 830-997-8600 *Web:* www.pacificwarmuseum.org *Email:* info@nimitzfoundation.org *Visitors welcome?* Yes *Hours:* Wednesday to Sunday, 11 a.m. to 3 p.m. *Admission:* $18 adults, $14 seniors, $8 students/children six to 17, five and under FREE *Operated by:* Admiral Nimitz Foundation *NR?* No *NHL?* No *Built:* 1938 *Latitude:* 30.2722 *Longitude:* -98.8682

KAITEN (HACKENSACK, NJ)

The Japanese Kaiten suicide torpedo is on display as a dry-berth exhibit at the closed New Jersey Naval Museum. *Address:* 78 River St. *City:* Hackensack *State:* NJ *Zip:* 07601 *Phone:* 201-342-3268 *Visitors welcome?* Yes *Hours:* Contact attraction directly *Admission:* Contact attraction directly *Operated by:* Submarine Memorial Association **NR?** **Yes** *NHL?* No *Latitude:* 40.8805 *Longitude:* -74.0415

KAITEN (HONOLULU, HI)

The Imperial Japanese Navy one-man submarine Kaiten is a dry-berth exhibit at the USS Bowfin memorial display. *Address:* 11 Arizona Memorial Drive *City:* Honolulu *State:* HI *Zip:* 96818 *Phone:* 808-423-1341 *Web:* www.bowfin.org *Email:* info@bowfin.org *Visitors welcome?* Yes *Hours:* Daily, 7 a.m. to 5 p.m. *Admission:* $20 adults, $12 children four to 12, under four permitted in museum but not submarine *Operated by:* Pacific Fleet Submarine Memorial Association *NR?* No *NHL?* No *Latitude:* 21.3643 *Longitude:* -157.9380

LING

Launched in 1943, the World War II-era submarine USS Ling is planned for a floating exhibit at the Louisville Naval Museum. *Address:* *City:* Louisville *State:* KY *Visitors welcome?* No *Web:* www.njnm.org/index.html *Email:* NJNavalMuseum@yahoo.com

Hours: Contact attraction directly *Admission:* Contact attraction directly *Operated by:* Submarine Memorial Association **NR? Yes** *NHL?* No *Built:* 1943 *Latitude:* 40.8805 *Longitude:* -74.0415

LIONFISH

Launched in 1944, the World War II-era submarine USS Lionfish is a floating exhibit at Battleship Cove. *Address:* 5 Water St. *City:* Fall River *State:* MA *Zip:* 02722 *Phone:* 508-678-1100 Toll-free: 800-533-3194 *Web:* www.battleshipcove.org *Visitors welcome?* Yes *Hours:* Daily, 9 a.m. to 5 p.m. *Admission:* $25 adults, $23 seniors, $16 active military, $15 children four to 12, children three and under FREE *Operated by:* Battleship Cove **NR? Yes NHL? Yes** *Built:* 1944 *Latitude:* 41.7040 *Longitude:* -71.1597

PAMPANITO

Launched in 1943, the World War II-era submarine USS Pampanito is now a museum ship on the San Francisco waterfront. *Address:* Fisherman's Wharf *City:* San Francisco *State:* CA *Zip:* 94133 *Phone:* 415-775-1943 *Web:* www.maritime.org *Visitors welcome?* Yes *Hours:* Daily, 9 a.m. to 5 p.m. *Admission:* $15 adults *Operated by:* San Francisco Maritime National Park Association **NR? Yes NHL? Yes** *Built:* 1943 *Latitude:* 37.8067 *Longitude:* -122.4110

RAZORBACK

Launched in 1944, the World War II-era submarine USS Razorback is a floating museum. *Address:* 120 Riverfront Park Dr. *City:* North Little Rock *State:* AR *Zip:* 72114 *Phone:* 501-371-8320 *Web:* aimmuseum.org *Email:* info@aimmuseum.org *Visitors welcome?* Yes *Hours:* Wednesday to Saturday, 10 a.m. to 6 p.m.; Sunday, 1 p.m. to 6 p.m. *Admission:* $10 adults, $7.50 seniors and active military, $5 children 5-12 *Operated by:* Arkansas Inland Maritime Museum *NR?* No *NHL?* No *Built:* 1944 *Latitude:* 34.7541 *Longitude:* -92.2681

REQUIN

Launched in 1945, the World War II-era submarine USS Requin is a floating exhibit on the Pittsburgh riverfront. *Address:* One Allegheny Ave. *City:* Pittsburgh *State:* PA *Zip:* 15212 *Phone:* 412-237-3400 *Web:* www.carnegiesciencecenter.org *Visitors welcome?* Yes *Hours:*

Wednesday to Monday, 10 a.m. to 5 p.m. *Admission:* $19.95 adults, $14.95 seniors, $11.95 children, children under three FREE *Operated by:* Carnegie Science Center *NR?* No *NHL?* No *Built:* 1945 *Latitude:* 40.4518 *Longitude:* -80.0059

SEEHUND (HACKENSACK, NJ)

The World War II-era German Navy Seehund midget submarine is a dry-berth display at the New Jersey Naval Museum. *Address:* 78 River St. *City:* Hackensack *State:* NJ *Zip:* 07601 *Visitors welcome?* No *Hours:* Contact attraction directly *Admission:* Contact attraction directly *Operated by:* Submarine Memorial Association *NR?* No *NHL?* No *Latitude:* 40.8805 *Longitude:* -74.0415

SEEHUND (QUINCY, MA)

The Seehund is an example of World War II-era German Navy midget submarine. *Address:* 739 Washington Street *City:* Quincy *State:* MA *Zip:* 02169 *Phone:* 617-479-7900 *Web:* www.uss-salem.org *Email:* awebteam@uss-salem.org *Visitors welcome?* Yes *Hours: Hours:* Contact attraction directly *Admission:* $12 adults, $10 seniors, veterans, children 4-12, children under four FREE *Operated by:* United States Naval Shipbuilding Museum *NR?* No *NHL?* No *Latitude:* 42.2452 *Longitude:* -70.9700

SILURO SAN BARTOLOMEO

The World War II-era submersible Siluro San Bartolomeo is an Italian craft designed for commando operations. It is now a dry-berth exhibit at the Submarine Force Museum. *Address:* Naval Submarine Base New London *City:* Groton *State:* CT *Zip:* 06349 *Phone:* 860-694-3174 *Web:* www.ussnautilus.org *Email:* info@nautilus.org *Visitors welcome?* Yes *Hours:* May 1 to Sept. 30: Daily, 9 a.m. to 5 p.m.; Winter: Nov. 1 to April 30, daily, 9 a.m. to 4 p.m. *Admission:* FREE *Operated by:* Naval History & Heritage Command *NR?* No *NHL?* No *Latitude:* 41.3499 *Longitude:* -72.0759

SILVERSIDES

Launched in 1941, the World War II-era submarine USS Silversides is a floating exhibit at the Great Lakes Naval Memorial & Museum. *Address:* 1346 Bluff Street *City:* Muskegon *State:* MI *Zip:* 49441 *Phone:*

231-755-1230 *Web:* silversidesmuseum.org *Email:* contactus@silversidesmuseum.org *Visitors welcome?* Yes *Hours:* January to April: Monday to Friday, 10 a.m. to 4 p.m.; May to October: Daily, 10 a.m. to 5:30 p.m. *Admission:* Contact attraction directly *Operated by:* Great Lakes Naval Memorial & Museum **NR? Yes NHL? Yes** *Built:* 1941 *Latitude:* 43.2273 *Longitude:* -86.3368

TORSK

USS Torsk was launched in late 1944 and represented the state-of-the-art U.S. submarine technology in World War II. *Address:* Pier 3, Baltimore Inner Harbor (301 E. Pratt St.) *City:* Baltimore *State:* MD *Zip:* 21202 *Phone:* 410-539-1797 *Web:* www.historicships.org *Email:* administration@historicships.org *Visitors welcome?* Yes *Hours:* Contact attraction directly *Admission:* $15 adults, $13 seniors/students, $7 children six to 14, children five and under FREE *Operated by:* Historic Ships in Baltimore **NR? Yes NHL? Yes** *Built:* 1944 *Latitude:* 39.2866 *Longitude:* -76.6087

U-505

Launched in 1941, the World War II-era submarine U-505 is now a dry-berth exhibit at the Chicago Museum of Science and Industry. *Address:* 57th Street and Lake Shore Drive *City:* Chicago *State:* IL *Zip:* 60637 *Phone:* 773-684-1414 *Web:* www.msichicago.org *Email:* contact@msichicago.org *Visitors welcome?* Yes *Hours:* Wednesday to Sunday, 9:30 a.m. to 5:30 p.m. *Admission:* $21.95 adults, $12.95 children three to 11, children under three FREE *Operated by:* Museum of Science and Industry **NR? Yes NHL? Yes** *Built:* 1941 *Latitude:* 41.7925 *Longitude:* -87.5802.

Tugboats

ANGELS GATE

Launched in 1944, the World War II-era tugboat Angels Gate is an operational display at the Los Angeles Maritime Museum. *Address:* Berth 84, Foot of 6th St. *City:* San Pedro *State:* CA *Zip:* 90731 *Phone:* 310-548-7618 *Web:* www.lamaritimemuseum.org *Visitors welcome?* Yes *Hours:* Contact attraction directly *Admission:* Contact attraction directly *Operated by:* Los Angeles Maritime Museum *NR?* No *NHL?*

No *Built:* 1944 *Latitude:* 33.7387 *Longitude:* -118.2790

HOGA

Launched in May 1941, the service tug USS Hoga took part in the defense of Pearl Harbor on December 7, 1941. *Address:* 120 Riverfront Park Dr. *City:* North Little Rock *State:* AR *Zip:* 72114 *Phone:* 501-371-8320 *Web:* aimmuseum.org *Email:* info@aimmuseum.org *Visitors welcome?* Yes *Hours:* Wednesday to Saturday, 10 a.m. to 6 p.m.; Sunday, 1 p.m. to 6 p.m. *Admission:* $10 adults, $7.50 seniors and active military, $5 children 5-12 *Operated by:* Arkansas Inland Maritime Museum **NR? Yes NHL? Yes** *Built:* 1941 *Latitude:* 34.7541 *Longitude:* -92.2681

MAJOR ELISHA K. HENSON

Launched in 1943, the World War II-era tug Major Elisha K. Henson, also known as LT-5, is a floating exhibit at the H. Lee White Marine Museum. *Address:* West 1st Street Pier *City:* Oswego *State:* NY *Zip:* 13126 *Phone:* 315-342-0480 *Web:* www.hleewhitemarinemuseum.com *Email:* info@hleewhitemarinemuseum.com *Visitors welcome?* Yes *Hours:* Daily, 10 a.m. to 5 p.m. *Admission:* $8 adults, $4 youth, children 12 and under FREE *Operated by:* H. Lee White Marine Museum **NR? Yes NHL? Yes** *Built:* 1943 *Latitude:* 43.4553 *Longitude:* -76.5105

PRESSED FOR TIME? FYDDEYE RECOMMENDS	
All aircraft carriers	Typically open and easy to find
All battleships	Most have tours and docents
Cassin Young	Well-preserved destroyer
Pampanito	Near other historic vessels

2

WARSHIPS: PRE-20TH CENTURY

USS Constitution fires a 21-gun salute during the ship's annual Fourth of July turnaround cruise in Boston Harbor on July 4, 2013.

Most warships from the 18th and 19th centuries come from archaeological digs, but a few have survived almost intact. One, USS Constitution, is the oldest commissioned warship in the U.S. Navy.

CAIRO

Launched in 1862, the remains of the ironclad USS Cairo were raised in 1964. They are now part of the Vicksburg National Military Park. The engines and boilers have been designated National Historic Mechanical Engineering Landmarks by the American Society of

Mechanical Engineers. *Address:* Vicksburg National Military Park *City:* Vicksburg *State:* MS *Zip:* 39183-3495 *Phone:* 601-636-0583 *Web:* www.nps.gov/vick/ *Visitors welcome?* Yes *Hours:* Daily, 8 a.m. to 5 p.m. *Admission:* FREE *Operated by:* Vicksburg National Military Park *NR?* No *NHL?* No *Built:* 1862 *Latitude:* 32.3731 *Longitude:* -90.8508

CHATTAHOOCHEE

Launched in 1862, the remains of the Civil War gunboat CSS Chattahoochee are on display at the National Civil War Naval Museum. *Address:* 1002 Victory Drive *City:* Columbus *State:* GA *Zip:* 31901 *Phone:* 706-327-9798 *Web:* www.portcolumbus.org *Email:* director@portcolumbus.org *Visitors welcome?* Yes *Hours:* Monday to Saturday, 10 a.m. to 4:30 p.m., Sunday, 12:30 p.m. to 4:30 p.m. *Admission:* $8 adults, $7 seniors/active military, $6 students *Operated by:* National Civil War Naval Museum **NR? Yes** *NHL?* No *Built:* 1862 *Latitude:* 32.4475 *Longitude:* -84.9792

CONSTELLATION

Built in 1854, USS Constellation is the last all-sail ship built by the U.S. Navy that is still afloat. *Address:* Pier 1, Baltimore Inner Harbor (301 E. Pratt St.) *City:* Baltimore *State:* MD *Zip:* 21202 *Phone:* 410-539-1797 *Web:* www.historicships.org *Email:* administration@historicships.org *Visitors welcome?* Yes *Hours:* Contact attraction directly *Admission:* $15 adults, $13 seniors/students, $7 children six to 14, children five and under FREE *Operated by:* Historic Ships in Baltimore **NR? Yes NHL? Yes** *Built:* 1854 *Latitude:* 39.2866 *Longitude:* -76.6087

CONSTITUTION

Nicknamed Old Ironsides for its strong wooden hull, the USS Constitution is the oldest commissioned warship in the U.S. Navy and a premier example of the nation's maritime heritage. *Address:* Constitution Road *City:* Boston *State:* MA *Zip:* 02129 *Phone:* 617-242-7511 *Web:* ussconstitutionmuseum.org *Visitors welcome?* Yes *Hours:* Contact attraction directly *Admission:* FREE *Operated by:* Naval History & Heritage Command *NR?* No *NHL?* No *Built:* 1797 *Latitude:* 42.3720 *Longitude:* -71.0595

H.L. HUNLEY

Wrecked on Feb. 17, 1864, the Civil War-era submarine H.L. Hunley is undergoing conservation at the Warren Lasch Conservation Center in the former Charleston Navy Yard. *Address:* 1250 Supply St. *City:* North Charleston *State:* SC *Zip:* 29405 *Phone:* 843-743-4865 *Web:* www.hunley.org *Email:* info@hunley.org *Visitors welcome?* Yes *Hours:* Contact attraction directly *Admission:* Contact attraction directly *Operated by:* Friends of the Hunley *NR?* No *NHL?* No *Built:* 1863 *Latitude:* 32.8563 *Longitude:* -79.9583

INTELLIGENT WHALE

Launched in 1865, the Civil War submarine Intelligent Whale is a dry-berth exhibit at the Sea Girt campus of the National Guard Militia Museum of New Jersey. *Address:* 66 Camp Drive *City:* Sea Girt *State:* NJ *Zip:* 08750 *Phone:* 732-974-5966 *Web:* njmilitiamuseum.org *Email:* carol.fowler@dmava.nj.gov *Visitors welcome?* Yes *Hours:* Monday to Friday, 10 a.m. to 3 p.m. *Admission:* Contact attraction directly *Operated by:* National Guard Militia Museum of New Jersey *NR?* No *NHL?* No *Built:* 1865 *Latitude:* 40.1298 *Longitude:* -74.0423

JACKSON

Launched in 1864, the remains of the ironclad ram CSS Jackson are on display at the National Civil War Naval Museum. *Address:* 1002 Victory Drive *City:* Columbus *State:* GA *Zip:* 31901 *Phone:* 706-327-9798 *Web:* www.portcolumbus.org *Email:* director@portcolumbus.org *Visitors welcome?* Yes *Hours:* Monday to Saturday, 10 a.m. to 4:30 p.m., Sunday, 12:30 p.m. to 4:30 p.m. *Admission:* $8 adults, $7 seniors/active military, $6 students *Operated by:* National Civil War Naval Museum *NR?* No *NHL?* No *Built:* 1864 *Latitude:* 32.4475 *Longitude:* -84.9792

MONITOR

Launched in 1862, the Civil War-era USS Monitor was the first ironclad ship to be commissioned in the U.S. Navy. The remains are now in the USS Monitor Center at the Mariners Museum in Norfolk, Virginia. *Address:* 100 Museum Drive *City:* Newport News *State:* VA *Zip:* 23606 *Phone:* 757-596-2222 *Web:* www.mariner.org *Visitors welcome?* Yes *Hours:* Contact attraction directly *Admission:* Contact attraction directly *Operated by:* Mariners Museum *NR?* No *NHL?* No *Built:* 1862 *Latitude:* 37.0420 *Longitude:* -76.4882

OLYMPIA

Launched in 1892, the cruiser USS Olympia is the oldest steel-hulled warship afloat in the world. Decommissioned in 1922, the Olympia is now an exhibit at the Independence Seaport Museum. *Address:* 211 South Columbus Blvd. *City:* Philadelphia *State:* PA *Zip:* 19106 *Phone:* 215-413-8655 *Web:* www.phillyseaport.org *Email:* seaport@phillyseaport.org *Visitors welcome?* Yes *Hours:* Thursday to Saturday, 10 a.m. to 5 p.m., Sunday, noon to 5 p.m. *Admission:* $18 adults; $10 seniors; $14 children, seniors, military; children under two FREE *Operated by:* Independence Seaport Museum **NR? Yes NHL? Yes** *Built:* 1892 *Latitude:* 39.9457 *Longitude:* -75.1419

PHILADELPHIA

Launched in 1776, the gunboat Philadelphia is a dry-berth exhibit in the Smithsonian's National Museum of American History. *Address:* 12th and Constitution Ave. NW *City:* Washington *State:* DC *Zip:* 20560 *Phone:* 202-357-1300 *Web:* americanhistory.si.edu *Visitors welcome?* Yes *Hours:* Friday to Tuesday, 11 a.m. to 4 p.m. *Admission:* Contact attraction directly *Operated by:* Smithsonian Institution **NR? Yes NHL? Yes** *Built:* 1776 *Latitude:* 38.8921 *Longitude:* -77.0280

PRESSED FOR TIME? FYDDEYE RECOMMENDS	
Constitution	Oldest commissioned warship
Monitor	Turning point in maritime history

3

WARSHIPS: WORLD WAR I &
POST-WORLD WAR II

The PBR (Patrol Boat, River) was the workhorse of the "brown water navy" during the Vietnam War. (Photo: Submarine Memorial Association)

Only one major warship built in World War I has survived to this day: USS Texas. In the period after World War II, including the Cold War, a handful of capital ships are preserved. In the case of the Vietnam War, most preserved boats were designed to patrol the country's major rivers.

PBR: The Most Famous Small Boat You've Never Heard Of

By Joe Follansbee

In the spring of 1979, just a few years after the end of the Vietnam War, hundreds of thousands of Americans watched a small boat cruising on a river. Hollywood had just released Apocalypse Now, an epic story of a US solder on the hunt for a rogue officer. The officer traveled up the Mekong River in a PBR, a US Navy acronym for "patrol boat, river." The film re-enacted a scene most American film-goers had never heard witnessed, a journey on a hostile waterway among a hidden enemy. Americans knew the story of land battles and ambushes, but they had never seen a patrol by the "brown water navy."

The guerrilla nature of warfare in Vietnam required the Navy to add innovative watercraft to its arsenal and fight far inland on the country's maze of rivers. Battleships and jet aircraft were little use against irregular units using sampans and junks to ferry supplies and fighters on the country's river highways. In 1966, the first eleven examples of a new kind of small craft arrived at Cat Lo, a major US naval combat and logistics base on the northern shore of Cape Vung Tau. The PBR was a high-speed, shallow draft, diesel-powered freshwater patrol craft with a fiberglass hull and water jet propulsion, instead of the standard metal or wood hull and propellers. The PBR was the first jet-propelled watercraft used in combat and it became an integral part of the "brown water navy," the informal name of the units that sailed Vietnam's silty rivers. The boats were placed under the control of Task Force 116, also known as Operation Game Warden.

Game Warden forces were charged with disrupting the insurgents known as the "Viet Cong." Game Warden units performed harassment and interdiction operations, river patrols, and minesweeping operations, especially along the main shipping channels around Saigon, now called Ho Chi Minh City. They were authorized to visit and search all river craft, except treaty-protected, foreign-flagged steel-hull merchant ships, warships, and military, police or customs craft.

The PBR became the main tool for Game Warden. The 11 boats delivered in March 1966 and the approximately 300 delivered over the next few years to the US and South Vietnamese military were based on a pleasure boat design constructed by Uniflite, a boatyard in Bellingham, Washington, located on the northern end of Puget Sound near the Canadian border. In October 1965, the Navy awarded a contract to the company for construction of 140 PBRs. The first craft off the assembly line, called the Mark I, was 31 feet long with a hull constructed entirely of fiberglass, a technology developed in the early 1950s. Powered by twin, 250-horsepower, 318-cubic-inch Detroit Allison 6v-53 diesel engines, the vessel cruised at 25 to 32 knots, extremely high-speed for a naval craft at the time. At idle, the engines made a warm, low thrum-thrum sound. The 9.5-ton vessels had a range of 150 nautical miles at 25 knots.

The boat's nine-inch draft and innovative propulsion made it ideal for operations in shallow, slow-moving water. Instead of propellers, the engines drove pumps built by the Jacuzzi Corporation, which later gained fame in the spa and health club market. Gushing at 6,000 gallons a minute through nozzles six inches in diameter, the water jets powered the boats over shallow water almost as easily as deep water. Some operators said the boats could skip over small mud flats and run at speed in six inches of water. Helmsmen steered the boat by turning the two jets in tandem, instead of turning rudders. This meant incredible maneuverability; the boat could perform a 180-degree turn in a boat length.

Given their purpose as fast and light patrol boats, PBRs had relatively limited armor and weaponry. The hull was completely unarmored, though the lack of protection was rarely a problem. Crewmen reported that rocket-propelled grenades would sometimes pass through the fiberglass without exploding, leaving just a small hole. (On other boats, an exploding warhead shredded metal or wood hulls, often causing as much damage to personnel as the warhead itself.) And the holes could be easily repaired with patch kits. A small amount of steel armor was placed around the helmsman's station.

The PBRs came equipped with a twin, .50 caliber M-36 machine gun turret in the bow, a single M1919AH .30 caliber machine gun in the stern, and an M-60 or an M-18 rapid fire grenade launcher. Four men manned the vessel: a boat captain (E5-E6 petty officer), an engineman (E4-E5 petty officer), a gunners mate (E4-E5 petty officer), and a seaman (E2-E3 sailor). The crew carried M-16 rifles and .45 caliber sidearms. Crewmen also operated a Raytheon 1900 radar unit and two URC-46 radios. A fifth person, often a South Vietnamese police officer or customs officer, sometimes accompanied the boats on patrols.

The Navy experienced problems with the Mark I PBRs within a few months of delivery. Crews noticed premature aging, corrosion and deterioration of the hull. Cracks allowed water to invade the Styrofoam hull reinforcement. The cracks were apparently caused by repeated hoisting and lowering in moderate seas and heavy weather. The Jacuzzi pumps also aged quickly in the harsh conditions. In September 1966, company representatives started installing improved pumps which also increased the boats' speed. They also recommended that divers frequently clear the pump intakes of rice, fish, grass, weeds, and the occasional snake. The long patrol hours meant little time for maintenance, and spare parts were at a premium, and the boats could be noisy. On a quiet night, PBRs running at high-speed could be heard more than three miles away.

In 1967, a second version of the PBR appeared, the Mark II, with aluminum gunwales installed to protect the sides of the boat when junks and sampans came alongside. A transom was also installed, lengthening the boat by about six inches, along with numerous superficial changes. Approximately 418 Mark II PBRs were constructed by Uniflite, and most of the inventory was delivered to the theater of operations. A number of the boats were also sold to foreign navies, including the Philippines Navy, or to domestic police forces. A Philippines Navy PBR appeared as a US Navy PBR in the film *Apocalypse Now*.

PBR tactics were tailored to the vessel's strengths and weaknesses. Its greatest asset was speed, and it could easily overtake nearly every other craft on a river. By the same token, it could also outrun practically anything the enemy could offer. Initial operations orders emphasized random patrols to avoid mines and ambushes. Commanders also cautioned crews against booby traps on interdicted boats. Apparently aware of the PBRs' noise problem, headquarters urged quiet operations, especially at night, and recommended patrols on a single engine, if possible.

PBRs played limited roles in offensive operations, although they would set ambushes at suspected VC river crossings. PBRs also assisted with psychological operations, dropping leaflets and playing taped broadcasts urging cooperation among local people. Crews also distributed food items to local villages.

While the PBR was primarily a weapon in the Navy's arsenal, the Army also made use of the vessel. On October 13, 1966, the 458th Transportation Company (10th Battalion, 4th Transportation Command) arrived at Cam Ranh Bay supply base, and at the time, it was the Army's only logistical amphibious unit in the operating theater. The unit's missions included harbor patrol and security at several ports, and in early 1968, it received its first allotment of 39 Mark II PBRs. Renamed the 458th Transportation Company (PBR), the unit became the only PBR company in the US Army. The Army boats were called "J-Boats" to distinguish them from their Navy cousins.

As the war wound down, Army and Navy PBRs were turned over to the Vietnamese government. At least one boat made it back to the states, a Mark I that served near Hue on the Perfume River. This boat is now in the collection of the Bellingham Museum of Maritime History. Other historical organizations, such as Gamewardens NW, a Vietnam veterans group, operate restored PBRs, and display them at community events. parades, and holidays commemorating the soldiers and sailors who served in them.

Joe Follansbee is the editor of The Fyddeye Guides. A version of this article first appeared in Vietnam *magazine.*

Warships - World War I

TEXAS

Launched in 1914, the World War I and II-era battleship USS Texas is now a floating museum at San Jacinto Battleground State Park. *Address:* 3527 Battleground Rd. *City:* La Porte *State:* TX *Zip:* 77571 *Phone:* 281-479-2431 *Web:* www.battleshiptexas.org *Email:* info@battleshiptexas.org *Visitors welcome?* Yes *Hours:* Contact attraction directly *Admission:* Contact attraction directly *Operated by:* Battleship Texas Foundation **NR? Yes NHL? Yes** *Built:* 1914 *Latitude:* 29.7311 *Longitude:* -95.0838

Warships – Post-World War II

ARIES

Launched in 1982, the guided missile hydrofoil gunboat USS Aries is a now a museum ship. *Address:* 1495 Corp Road *City:* Morrison *State:* MO *Zip:* 65061 *Phone:* 636-541-6130 *Web:* www.ussaries.org *Visitors welcome?* Yes *Hours:* Contact attraction directly *Admission:* Contact attraction directly *Operated by:* USS Aries Hydrofoil Memorial *NR?* No *NHL?* No *Built:* 1982 *Latitude:* 38.6695 *Longitude:* -91.5602

BARC 3-X

Launched in 1952, BARC (Barge, Amphibious Resupply, Cargo) 3-X is a dry berth exhibit at the U.S. Army Transportation Museum in Fort Eustis. The BARC, and a later version, LARC (Lighter, Amphibious Resupply, Cargo), were welded, steel-hulled amphibious cargo vehicles. *Address:* 300 Washington Blvd., Besson Hall *City:* Fort Eustis *State:* VA *Zip:* 23604-5260 *Phone:* 757-878-1115 *Web:* transportation.army.mil/museum *Email:* atmuseumfoundation@gmail.com *Visitors welcome?* Yes *Hours:* Contact attraction directly *Operated by:* U.S. Army Transportation Museum *NR?* No *NHL?* No *Built:* 1952 *Latitude:* 37.1585 *Longitude:* -76.5844

BAYLANDER

Launched in 1968, the helicopter landing training ship USS Baylander is now a museum ship at the West Harlem Piers in New York City. *Address:* West Harlem Piers *City:* New York *State:* NY *Zip:* 10027 *Phone:* 917-280-3934 *Web:* www.baylander.nyc *Visitors welcome?* Yes *Hours:* Contact attraction directly *Admission:* Contact attraction directly *NR?* No *NHL?* No *Latitude:* 40.8191 *Longitude:* -73.9645

CCB-18

The command-and-control boat CCB-18 is a dry-berth exhibit at Naval Amphibious Base Coronado. *Address:* Tulagi Rd., Naval Amphibious Base Coronado *City:* Coronado *State:* CA *Zip:* 92118 *Web:* www.vummf.org *Hours:* Daily *Admission:* FREE *Operated by:* Vietnam Unit Memorial Monument *NR?* No *NHL?* No *Latitude:* 32.6740 *Longitude:* -117.161299

DSU DIVE BOAT

Launched in 1968, the Deep Submergence Unit (DSU) Dive Boat was originally designed to land tanks, but later converted to a vessel used for salvage, rescue or training. *City:* Sacramento *State:* CA *Zip:* 95833 *Phone:* 916-715-0563 *Web:* libertymaritime.com *Email:* liberty-maritime@msn.com *Visitors welcome?* Yes *Hours:* Contact attraction directly *Admission:* Contact attraction directly *Operated by:* Liberty Maritime Museum *NR?* No *NHL?* No *Built:* 1968 *Latitude:* 38.6051 *Longitude:* -121.5240

EDSON

Launched in 1958, the destroyer USS Edson is a floating exhibit on the Bay City waterfront. *Address:* Philadelphia Navy Yard *City:* Bay City *State:* MI *Zip:* 48706 *Phone:* 989-684-3946 *Web:* www.ussedson.org *Email:* info@ussedson.org *Visitors welcome?* Yes *Hours:* Contact attraction directly *Admission:* Contact attraction directly *Operated by:* Saginaw Valley Naval Ship Museum **NR? Yes NHL? Yes** *Built:* 1958 *Latitude:* 43.5945 *Longitude:* -83.8889

FRESH-1

The hydrofoil FRESH-1 was a U.S. Navy research vessel. *Address:* 1495 Corp Road *City:* Morrison *State:* MO *Zip:* 65061 *Phone:* 636-541-

6130 *Web:* www.ussaries.org *Visitors welcome?* Yes *Hours:* Contact attraction directly *Admission:* Contact attraction directly *Operated by:* USS Aries Hydrofoil Memorial *NR?* No *NHL?* No *Built:* 1982 *Latitude:* 38.6695 *Longitude:* -91.5602

HIDDENSEE

Launched in 1985, the Russian-built missile corvette Hiddensee is a floating exhibit at Battleship Cove. *Address:* Five Water Street *City:* Fall River *State:* MA *Zip:* 02722-0111 *Phone:* 508-678-1100 *Web:* www.battleshipcove.org *Email:* battleship@battleshipcove.org *Visitors welcome?* Yes *Hours:* Daily, 9 a.m. to 5 p.m. *Admission:* $25 adults, $23 seniors, $16 active military, $15 children four to 12, children three and under FREE *Operated by:* Battleship Cove *NR?* No *NHL?* No *Built:* 1985 *Latitude:* 41.7040 *Longitude:* -71.1597

J-3795

Launched in 1954, the passenger launch J-3795 is now a dry-berth exhibit at the U.S. Army Transportation Museum. *Address:* 300 Washington Blvd., Besson Hall *City:* Fort Eustis *State:* VA *Zip:* 23604 *Phone:* 757-878-1115 *Web:* transportation.army.mil/museum *Email:* atmuseumfoundation@gmail.com *Visitors welcome?* Yes *Hours:* Contact attraction directly *Operated by:* U.S. Army Transportation Museum *NR?* No *NHL?* No *Built:* 1954 *Latitude:* 37.1585 *Longitude:* -76.5844

LUCID

Launched in 1953, the minesweeper USS Lucid is now a museum ship on Bradford Island, Calif. *Address:* 4290 Cherokee Road *City:* Stockton *State:* CA *Phone:* 877-285-8243 *Web:* stocktonhistoricalmaritimemuseum.org *Email:* shmm.info@gmail.com *Visitors welcome?* Yes *Hours:* Contact attraction directly *Admission:* Contact attraction directly *Operated by:* Lucid MSO-458 Foundation *NR?* No *NHL?* No *Built:* 1953 *Latitude:* 75.5401 *Longitude:* -101.3790

PACV-4

Launched in 1965, the hovercraft PACV-4 is a dry-berth exhibit at the Bellingham International Maritime Museum. *Address:* 800

Cornwall Ave. *City:* Bellingham *State:* WA *Zip:* 98225 *Phone:* 360-592-4112 *Visitors welcome?* Yes *Hours:* Contact attraction directly *Admission:* Contact attraction directly *Operated by:* Bellingham International Maritime Museum *NR?* No *NHL?* No *Built:* 1965 *Latitude:* 48.7487 *Longitude:* -122.4810

PATROL BOAT, FAST

The Buffalo and Erie County Naval and Military Park collection include a Vietnam-era "patrol boat, fast" boat. *Address:* One Naval Park Cove *City:* Buffalo *State:* NY *Zip:* 14202 *Phone:* 716-847-1773 *Web:* www.buffalonavalpark.org *Email:* info@buffalonavalpark.org *Visitors welcome?* Yes *Hours:* Wednesday to Sunday, 10 a.m. to 5 p.m. *Admission:* $16 adults, $13 seniors, $12 veteran, $10 children five to 12, children under four FREE *Operated by:* Buffalo and Erie County Naval & Military Park *NR?* No *NHL?* No *Latitude:* 42.8994 *Longitude:* -78.8759

PBR (EVERETT, WA)

The PBR (Patrol Boat, River) was a riverine patrol craft first deployed in the early years of the Vietnam War and served throughout the conflict. Two versions, the Mark I and Mark II, were constructed in Bellingham, Wash. *City:* Everett *State:* WA *Web:* www.gamewardensnw.org *Email:* leadership@gamewardensnw.org *Phone:* 253-377-8007 *Visitors welcome?* Yes *Hours:* Contact attraction directly *Admission:* FREE *Operated by:* Gamewardens Northwest Chapter *NR?* No *NHL?* No *Built:* 1973 *Latitude:* 47.9790 *Longitude:* -122.2020

PBR 722 (BELLINGHAM, WA)

The Vietnam-era PBR (Patrol Boat, River) 722 is on display at the Bellingham International Maritime Museum. *Address:* 800 Cornwall Ave. *City:* Bellingham *State:* WA *Zip:* 98225 *Phone:* 360-592-4112 *Web:* www.pbr722.com *Visitors welcome?* Yes *Hours:* Contact attraction directly *Admission:* Contact attraction directly *Operated by:* Bellingham International Maritime Museum *NR?* No *NHL?* No *Latitude:* 48.7487 *Longitude:* -122.4810

PBR MARK I (MOUNT PLEASANT, SC)

The Mark I patrol boat, river (PBR) is a Vietnam-era river craft that supported ground operations. The craft is part of an exhibit that replicates a typical naval support base in South Vietnam. *Address:* 40 Patriots Point Road *City:* Mount Pleasant *State:* SC *Zip:* 29464 *Phone:* 843-884-2727 Toll-free: 866-831-1720 *Web:* www.patriotspoint.org *Visitors welcome?* Yes *Hours:* Daily, 9:30 a.m. to 6 p.m. *Admission:* $27 adults, $19 seniors, $16 children six to 11, under six FREE *Operated by:* Patriots Point Naval & Maritime Museum *NR?* No *NHL?* No *Latitude:* 32.7940 *Longitude:* -79.9051

PBR MARK II (BELLINGHAM, WA)

The Vietnam-era PBR (Patrol Boat, River) Mark II is on display at the Bellingham International Maritime Museum. *Address:* 800 Cornwall Ave. *City:* Bellingham *State:* WA *Zip:* 98225 *Phone:* 360-592-4112 *Visitors welcome?* Yes *Hours:* Contact attraction directly *Admission:* Contact attraction directly *Operated by:* Bellingham International Maritime Museum *NR?* No *NHL?* No *Latitude:* 48.7487 *Longitude:* -122.4810

PBR MARK II (MOBILE, AL)

The PBR Mark II was a river patrol boat developed for use in Vietnam. *Address:* Battleship Memorial Park *City:* Mobile *State:* AL *Zip:* 36601 *Phone:* 251-433-2703 *Web:* www.ussalabama.com *Email:* info@ussalabama.com *Visitors welcome?* Yes *Hours:* October to March, daily, 8 a.m. to 4 p.m.; April to Sept., daily, 8 a.m. to 6 p.m. *Admission:* $15 adults, $13 seniors, $6 children six to 11, under six FREE *Operated by:* Battleship Memorial Park **NR? Yes** *NHL?* No *Latitude:* 30.6818 *Longitude:* -88.0148

PBR MARK II (WASHINGTON, DC)

The patrol boat, river (PBR) Mark II, or "Pibber" is a 31-foot fiberglass-hulled patrol boat designed and produced by the United States to patrol inland river and "brown water" areas. *Address:* 805 Kidder Breese SE, Washington Navy Yard *City:* Washington *State:* DC *Zip:* 20374 *Phone:* 202-433-6897 *Web:* https://www.history.navy.mil/content/history/museums/nmusn.html *Visitors welcome?* Yes *Hours:* Monday to Friday, 9 a.m. to 4 p.m.,

Saturdays, 10 a.m. to 4 p.m. *Admission:* Contact attraction directly *Operated by:* National Museum of the United States Navy *NR?* No *NHL?* No *Built:* 1965 *Latitude:* 38.8755 *Longitude:* -76.9935

PBR MARK II (WEATHERFORD, TX)

The Vietnam-ear PBR (Patrol Boat, River) Mark II is a dry-berth display. *Address:* 12685 Mineral Wells Highway *City:* Weatherford *State:* TX *Zip:* 76086 *Phone:* 940-325-4003 *Web:* www.nationalvnwarmuseum.org *Email:* muleskinner3@verizon.net *Visitors welcome?* Yes *Hours:* Daily, 9 a.m. to 1 p.m., until 5 p.m. Tuesdays. *Admission:* Contact attraction directly *Operated by:* National Vietnam War Museum *NR?* No *NHL?* No *Latitude:* 32.7593 *Longitude:* -97.7973

PBR MARK II (VALLEJO, CA)

The Vietnam-ear PBR (Patrol Boat, River) Mark II is a dry-berth display at the Mare Island Historic Park museum in Vallejo. *Address:* 1100 Railroad Avenue *City:* Vallejo *State:* CA *Zip:* 94592 *Phone:* 707-557-4646 *Web:* www.mareislandmuseum.org *Email:* info@mareislandmuseum.org *Visitors welcome?* Yes *Hours:* Contact attraction directly *Admission:* Contact attraction directly *Operated by:* Mare Island Historic Park Foundation *NR?* No *NHL?* No *Latitude:* 38.0888 *Longitude:* -122.2710

PCF-1

Launched in 1965, PCF-1, also known as a Swift Boat, was a river patrol craft. It is now a dry-berth exhibit at the Washington Navy Yard. *Address:* 805 Kidder Breese SE, Washington Navy Yard *City:* Washington *State:* DC *Zip:* 20374 *Phone:* 202-433-6897 *Web:* https://www.history.navy.mil/content/history/museums/nmusn.html *Visitors welcome?* Yes *Hours:* Monday to Friday, 9 a.m. to 4 p.m., Saturdays, 10 a.m. to 4 p.m. *Admission:* Contact attraction directly *Operated by:* National Museum of the United States Navy *NR?* No *NHL?* No *Built:* 1965 *Latitude:* 38.8755 *Longitude:* -76.9935

PCF-104

The US Navy patrol craft, PCF-104, is a Vietnam-era river patrol boat and a dry-berth exhibit. *Address:* Tulagi Rd., Naval Amphibious

Base Coronado *City:* Coronado *State:* CA *Zip:* 92118 *Web:*
www.vummf.org *Hours:* Daily *Admission:* FREE *Operated by:* Vietnam
Unit Memorial Monument *NR?* No *NHL?* No *Latitude:* 32.6740
Longitude: -117.161299

PT-658

Launched in 1945, the fast patrol boat PT-658 is now a museum ship.
Address: Pier 307, Vigor Shipyard *City:* Portland *State:* OR *Phone:* 503-
286-3083 *Web:* www.savetheptboatinc.com *Email:*
ptboat658@gmail.com *Visitors welcome?* Yes *Hours:* Monday,
Thursday, Saturday, 9 a.m. to 3 p.m. *Admission:* By donation *Operated
by:* Save The PT Boat, Inc. *NR?* No *NHL?* No *Built:* 1945 *Latitude:*
45.5649 *Longitude:* -122.7191

*Remember to call first before visiting a smaller museum or historical
society. Many close on major holidays or display their small vessels at
community events.*

PTF-3

Launched in 1963, the fast patrol boat PTF-3 is undergoing
restoration by Boy Scout Troop 544. *Address:* Deland Naval Air
Station Museum, 910 Biscayne Blvd. *City:* Deland *State:* FL *Zip:* 32724
Phone: 386-738-4149 *Web:* www.ptf3restoration.org *Email:*
ptf3restore@embarqmail.com *Visitors welcome?* Yes *Hours:* Contact
attraction directly *Admission:* Contact attraction directly *Operated by:*
PTF 3 Restoration Project *NR?* No *NHL?* No *Built:* 1963 *Latitude:*
29.0576 *Longitude:* -81.2876

PTF-17

Launched in 1968, the Trumpy class, fast patrol boat PTF-17 is a dry-
berth exhibit. *Address:* One Naval Park Cove *City:* Buffalo *State:* NY
Zip: 14202 *Phone:* 716-847-1773 *Web:* www.buffalonavalpark.org
Email: info@buffalonavalpark.org *Visitors welcome?* Yes *Hours:*
Wednesday to Sunday, 10 a.m. to 5 p.m. *Admission:* $16 adults, $13
seniors, $12 veteran, $10 children five to 12, children under four
FREE *Operated by:* Buffalo and Erie County Naval & Military Park
NR? No *NHL?* No *Built:* 1968 *Latitude:* 42.8994 *Longitude:* -78.8759

PTF-26

Launched in 1968, PTF 26, called Liberty, is the last of the Fast Patrol Boats constructed. The vessel saw service in Vietnam. *City:* Sacramento *State:* CA *Zip:* 95833 *Phone:* 916-715-0563 *Web:* libertymaritime.com *Email:* liberty-maritime@msn.com *Visitors welcome?* Yes *Hours:* Contact attraction directly *Admission:* Contact attraction directly *Operated by:* Liberty Maritime Museum *NR?* No *NHL?* No *Built:* 1968 *Latitude:* 38.6051 *Longitude:* -121.5240

RECRUIT

Built in 1949, Recruit is a U.S. Navy training vessel, one of the few remaining "landships" built solely for training on land. *Address:* 4325-4461 N. Harbor Dr. *City:* San Diego *State:* CA *Zip:* 92101 *Visitors welcome?* *Hours:* Contact attraction directly *Admission:* Contact attraction directly No *NR?* **Yes** *NHL?* No *Operated by:* Liberty Station *Built:* 1949 *Latitude:* 32.7284 *Longitude:* -117.2163

SALEM

Launched in 1947, the heavy cruiser USS Salem is now a floating exhibit. *Address:* 739 Washington Street *City:* Quincy *State:* MA *Zip:* 02169 *Phone:* 617-479-7900 *Web:* www.uss-salem.org *Email:* awebteam@uss-salem.org *Visitors welcome?* Yes *Hours:* Contact attraction directly *Admission:* $12 adults, $10 seniors, veterans, children 4-12, children under four FREE *Operated by:* United States Naval Shipbuilding Museum *NR?* No *NHL?* No *Built:* 1947 *Latitude:* 42.2452 *Longitude:* -70.9700

TURNER JOY

Launched in 1957, the destroyer USS Turner Joy is now a floating museum on Puget Sound. *Address:* 300 Washington Ave. *City:* Bremerton *State:* WA *Phone:* 360-792-2457 *Web:* ussturnerjoy.org *Email:* dd951@ussturnerjoy.org *Visitors welcome?* Yes *Hours:* March to October: Daily, 10 a.m. to 5 p.m; November to February: Wednesday to Sunday, 10 a.m. to 4 p.m. *Admission:* $16 adults; $14 seniors, veterans; $11.50 children 13-17; $9.50 children five to 12; children four and under FREE *Operated by:* Bremerton Historic Ships Association *NR?* No *NHL?* No *Built:* 1957 *Latitude:* 47.5673 *Longitude:* -122.6240

Submarines

ALBACORE

Launched in 1953, the USS Albacore pioneered modern submarine technologies. The vessel is now dry-berthed as a museum. *Address:* Albacore Park, 600 Market Street *City:* Portsmouth *State:* NH *Zip:* 03801 *Phone:* 603-436-3680 *Web:* www.ussalbacore.org *Email:* info@ussalbacore.org *Visitors welcome?* Yes *Hours:* Saturday and Sunday, 9:30 a.m. to 4 p.m. *Admission:* FREE *Operated by:* Port of Portsmouth Maritime Museum **NR? Yes NHL? Yes** *Built:* 1953 *Latitude:* 43.0718 *Longitude:* -70.7626

B-39

Launched in the early 1970s, the Soviet attack submarine B-39 is a Cold War exhibit on display at the San Diego Maritime Museum. *Address:* 1492 North Harbor Drive *City:* San Diego *State:* CA *Zip:* 92101 *Phone:* 619-234-9153 *Web:* www.sdmaritime.com *Email:* info@sdmaritime.org *Visitors welcome?* Yes *Hours:* Daily, 10 a.m. to 8 p.m. *Admission:* $20 18+; $15 seniors, military, students; $10 children three to 12; children under two FREE *Operated by:* Maritime Museum Association of San Diego *NR?* No *NHL?* No *Built:* 1970 *Latitude:* 32.7276 *Longitude:* -117.1800

BLUEBACK

Launched in 1959, the submarine USS Blueback is on exhibit at the Oregon Museum of Science & Industry. *Address:* 1945 SE Water Avenue *City:* Portland *State:* OR *Zip:* 97214 *Phone:* 503-797-4624 *Web:* www.omsi.edu *Visitors welcome?* Yes *Hours:* Tuesday to Sunday, 10 a.m. to 5:30 p.m. *Admission:* $8.50 *Operated by:* Oregon Museum of Science & Industry *NR?* No *NHL?* No *Built:* 1959 *Latitude:* 45.5085 *Longitude:* -122.6660

DOLPHIN

Launched in 1968, the USS Dolphin was the last diesel-electric boat built for the US Navy. It's now at the San Diego Maritime Museum. *Address:* 1492 North Harbor Drive *City:* San Diego *State:* CA *Zip:* 92101 *Phone:* 619-234-9153 *Web:* www.sdmaritime.com *Email:* support@sdmaritime.org *Visitors welcome?* Yes *Hours:* Daily, 10 a.m. to

8 p.m. *Admission:* $20 18+; $15 seniors, military, students; $10 children three to 12; children under two FREE *Operated by:* Maritime Museum Association of San Diego **NR? Yes NHL? Yes** *Built:* 1898 *Latitude:* 32.7276 *Longitude:* -117.1800

GROWLER

Launched in 1954, the Cold War-era submarine USS Growler is a floating exhibit at the Intrepid Sea, Air & Space Museum in New York. *Address:* Pier 86, W. 46th St. and 12th Ave. *City:* New York *State:* NY *Zip:* 10036 *Phone:* 212-245-0072 Toll-free: 877-957-7447 *Web:* www.intrepidmuseum.org *Visitors welcome?* Yes *Hours:* Thursday to Sunday, 10 a.m. to 5 p.m. *Admission:* $33 adults; $31 seniors; $24 youth five to 12; under five FREE *Operated by:* Intrepid Sea-Air-Space Museum *NR?* No *NHL?* No *Built:* 1954 *Latitude:* 40.7631 *Longitude:* -73.9996

MARLIN

Launched in 1953, the target submarine USS Marlin is a dry-berth exhibit at Freedom Park in Omaha. *Address:* Freedom Park *City:* Omaha *State:* NE *Phone:* 402-444-7000 *Visitors welcome?* Yes *Hours:* Daily *Admission:* FREE *Operated by:* City of Omaha **NR? Yes** *NHL?* No *Built:* 1953 *Latitude:* 41.2716 *Longitude:* -95.9210

NAUTILUS

USS Nautilus was the world's first nuclear powered vessel, the first ship to go to the North Pole, and the first submarine to journey 20,000 leagues under the sea. The submarine is on exhibit at the Submarine Force Museum. *Address:* One Crystal Lake Rd. *City:* Groton *State:* CT *Zip:* 06340 *Phone:* 800-343-0079 *Web:* www.ussnautilus.org *Email:* info@nautilus.org *Visitors welcome?* Yes *Hours:* May 1 to Sept. 30: Daily, 9 a.m. to 5 p.m.; Winter: Nov. 1 to April 30, daily, 9 a.m. to 4 p.m. *Admission:* FREE *Operated by:* Naval History & Heritage Command *NR?* No *NHL?* No *Latitude:* 41.3499 *Longitude:* -72.0759

SCORPION

Launched in 1971, the Soviet Foxtrot-class submarine Scorpion is a floating exhibit berthed next to the Queen Mary in Long Beach.

Address: 1126 Queens Highway *City:* Long Beach *State:* CA *Zip:* 90802 *Phone:* 562-432-0424 *Visitors welcome?* No *Hours:* Contact attraction directly *Admission:* Contact attraction directly *Operated by:* Urban Commons *NR?* No *NHL?* No *Built:* 1971 *Latitude:* 33.7526 *Longitude:* -118.1900

X-1

Launched in 1955, the midget submarine X-1 is now a dry-berth exhibit at the Submarine Force Museum. *Address:* Naval Submarine Base New London *City:* Groton *State:* CT *Zip:* 06349 *Phone:* 860-694-3174 *Web:* www.ussnautilus.org *Email:* info@nautilus.org *Visitors welcome?* Yes *Hours: Hours:* May 1 to Sept. 30: Daily, 9 a.m. to 5 p.m.; Winter: Nov. 1 to April 30, daily, 9 a.m. to 4 p.m. *Admission:* FREE *Operated by:* Naval History & Heritage Command *NR?* No *NHL?* No *Built:* 1955 *Latitude:* 41.3499 *Longitude:* -72.0759

PRESSED FOR TIME? FYDDEYE RECOMMENDS	
PBR Mark I (Mt. Pleasant, SC)	Iconic "brown water navy" boat
Turner Joy	Early role in Vietnam War
Nautilus	Pioneering nuclear submarine

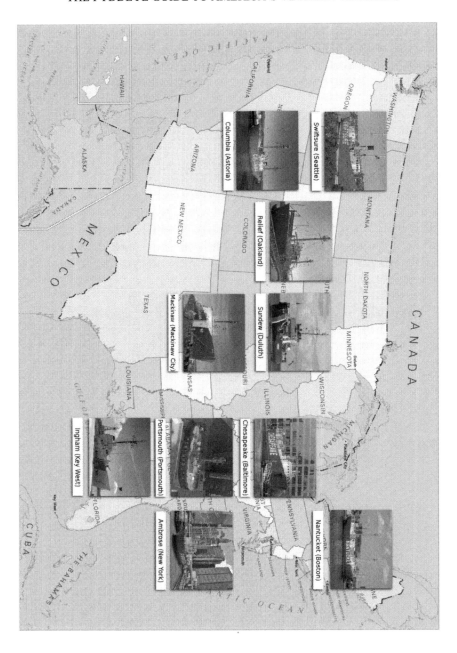

4

US COAST GUARD VESSELS

US Coast Guard icebreaker Mackinaw, now a museum, in Mackinaw City, Mich. (Photo: Peter K. Burian / Wikimedia Commons)

Though the mission of the Coast Guard is less military and more marine safety and the regulation of commercial traffic, Coast Guard vessels have played a vital role in preserving American freedoms.

ACACIA

Launched in 1944, the buoy tender USCGC Acacia is now an educational vessel in Manistee, Mich., next to the S.S. City of Milwaukee. *Address:* 99 Arthur Street *City:* Manistee *State:* MI *Zip:* 49660 *Phone:* 231-723-3587 *Web:* carferry.com *Email:* sscityofmilwaukee@gmail.com *Visitors welcome?* Yes *Hours:* Contact attraction directly *Admission:* Contact attraction directly *Operated by:* American Academy of Industry *NR?* No *NHL?* No *Built:* 1944 *Latitude:* 44.2595 *Longitude:* -86.3164

ARCTIC SCOUT

Launched in 1965, the Arctic survey boat USCGC Arctic Scout is an education and excursion vessel. *Address:* 757 SE 17th St. *City:* Fort Lauderdale *State:* FL *Zip:* 33316 *Phone:* 561-543-1288 *Web:* www.glaciersociety.org *Email:* groberts@glaciersociety.org *Visitors welcome?* Yes *Hours:* Contact attraction directly *Admission:* Contact attraction directly *Operated by:* Glacier Society *NR?* No *NHL?* No *Built:* 1965 *Latitude:* 26.1020 *Longitude:* -80.1201

CG 36500

Launched in 1946, the Coast Guard motor lifeboat CG 36500 is now a working exhibit owned by the Orleans Historical Society. *Address:* 3 River Road *City:* Orleans *State:* MA *Zip:* 02653 *Phone:* 508-240-1329 *Web:* www.orleanshistoricalsociety.org *Email:* admin@orleanshs.org *Visitors welcome?* Yes *Hours:* Contact attraction directly *Admission:* Contact attraction directly *Operated by:* Orleans Historical Society **NR? Yes** *NHL?* No *Built:* 1946 *Latitude:* 41.7832 *Longitude:* -69.9774

CG 52302D

Launched in 1944, the buoy boat CG 52302D is a dry-berth exhibit at the Lake Champlain Maritime Museum. *Address:* 4472 Basin Harbor Rd *City:* Vergennes *State:* VT *Zip:* 05491 *Phone:* 802-475-2022 *Web:* www.lcmm.org *Email:* info@lcmm.org *Visitors welcome?* Yes *Hours:* Contact attraction directly *Admission:* Contact attraction directly *Operated by:* Lake Champlain Maritime Museum *NR?* No *NHL?* No *Built:* 1944 *Latitude:* 44.1973 *Longitude:* -73.3567

CG 36460

The 36-foot Coast Guard motor lifeboat CG-36460 is an excursion vessel operated by the Michigan Maritime Museum. *Address:* 44720 Lighthouse Road *City:* Piney Point *State:* MD *Zip:* 20674 *Phone:* 301-994-1471 *Web:* www.stmarysmd.com/recreate/Museums *Visitors welcome?* Yes *Hours:* March 25 to October 31, Daily, 10 a.m. to 5 p.m. *Admission:* $7 adults, $3.50 seniors/students/active military, children under five FREE *Operated by:* St. Mary's County Museum Division *NR?* No *NHL?* No *Built:* 1941 *Latitude:* 38.1408 *Longitude:* -76.5202

CG-44385

The 44-foot motor lifeboat CG-44385 is in the collection of the Westport Maritime Museum awaiting restoration and display. *Address:* 2201 Westhaven Dr. *City:* Westport *State:* WA *Zip:* 98595 *Phone:* 360-268-0078 *Web:* www.westportmaritimemuseum.com *Visitors welcome?* Yes *Hours:* Thursday to Monday, 10 a.m. to 4 p.m. *Admission:* $5 adults, $3 children six to 16, $1 active and retired military, under six FREE *Operated by:* Westport Maritime Museum *NR?* No *NHL?* No *Latitude:* 46.9076 *Longitude:* - 124.1141

CG-83366

CG-83366 is the only remaining 83-foot cutter from Rescue Flotilla One. which served as a rescue vessel during the 1944 D-Day landings. She is currently undergoing restoration. *City:* Seattle *State:* WA *Phone:* 425-681-2311 *Web:* www.uscg11.org *Email:* uscgtiburon@gmail.com *Visitors welcome?* Yes *Hours:* Contact attraction directly *Admission:* Contact attraction directly *NR?* No *NHL?* No *Operated by:* US Coast Guard-11 / Tiburon / US Coast Guard-83366 Foundation *Built:* 1942 *Latitude:* 47.6131 *Longitude:* -122.4122

CG-83527

Launched in 1944, the World War II-era CG-83527 is now used as a living history and marine safety education vessel. *Address:* Swansonville Rd. and Oak Bay Rd. *City:* Port Ludlow *State:* WA *Web:* cg83527.org *Email:* at:83527@warboats.org *Visitors welcome?* Yes *Hours:* Contact attraction directly *Admission:* Contact attraction directly *Operated by:* Combatant Craft of America *NR?* No *NHL?* No *Built:* 1944 *Latitude:* 47.9294 *Longitude:* -122.6850

COMANCHE

Launched in 1944, the tug USCGC Comanche is undergoing restoration near Olympia, Wash. *Address:* 660 West Ewing St. *City:* Seattle *State:* WA *Zip:* 98119 *Phone:* 253-227-9678 *Web:* www.comanche202.org *Email:* ata202@live.com *Visitors welcome?* Yes

Hours: Contact attraction directly *Admission:* Contact attraction directly *Operated by:* Comanche 202 Foundation *NR?* No *NHL?* No *Built:* 1944 *Latitude:* 47.6528 *Longitude:* -122.3660

EAGLE

Launched in 1936, the barque USCGC Eagle is the sail-training vessel for the U.S. Coast Guard Academy. *Address:* 31 Mohegan Avenue *City:* New London *State:* CT *Zip:* 06320 *Phone:* 860-444-8444 *Web:* www.cga.edu *Visitors welcome?* Yes *Hours:* Contact attraction directly *Admission:* Contact attraction directly *Operated by:* U.S. Coast Guard Academy *NR?* No *NHL?* No *Built:* 1936 *Latitude:* 41.3703 *Longitude:* -72.1055

FIR

The lighthouse buoy tender USCGC Fir is undergoing restoration in Stockton, Calif. *Address:* West Eight Mile Road *City:* Stockton *State:* CA *Web:* fir212.com *Visitors welcome?* No *Hours:* Contact attraction directly *Admission:* Contact attraction directly *NR?* No **NHL? Yes** *Built:* 1939 *Latitude:* 38.0602 *Longitude:* -121.5016

INGHAM

Launched in 1936, the USCGC Ingham is now a floating exhibit. *Address:* Truman Waterfront *City:* Key West *State:* FL *Zip:* 33041 *Phone:* 305-395-9554 *Web:* www.uscgcingham.org *Email:* info@uscgcingham.org *Visitors welcome?* Yes *Hours:* Tuesday to Saturday, 10 a.m. to 4 p.m. *Admission:* $10 adults, $5 children seven to 12, children under six FREE *Operated by:* USCGC Ingham Maritime Museum **NR? Yes NHL? Yes** *Built:* 1936 *Latitude:* 24.5554 *Longitude:* -81.7828

MACKINAW

Launched in 1944 and decommissioned in 2006, the World War II-era icebreaker USCGC Mackinaw is now a museum ship. *Address:* 131 S. Huron Ave. *City:* Mackinaw City *State:* MI *Zip:* 49701 *Phone:* 231-436-9825 *Web:* www.themackinaw.org *Email:* info@themackinaw.org *Visitors welcome?* Yes *Hours:* May to October, 10 a.m. to 6 p.m. *Admission:* $12 adults, $6.50 youth six to 17, under five FREE *Operated by:* Icebreaker Mackinaw Maritime Museum *NR?*

No *NHL?* No *Built:* 1944 *Latitude:* 45.7821 *Longitude:* -84.7248

MCLANE

Launched in 1927, the USCGC McLane is a floating exhibit at the Silversides Museum. *Address:* 1346 Bluff Street *City:* Muskegon *State:* MI *Zip:* 49441 *Phone:* 231-755-1230 *Web:* silversidesmuseum.org *Email:* contactus@silversidesmuseum.org *Visitors welcome?* Yes *Hours:* January to April: Monday to Friday, 10 a.m. to 4 p.m.; May to October: Daily, 10 a.m. to 5:30 p.m. *Admission:* Contact attraction directly *Operated by:* Silversides Museum *NR?* No *NHL?* No *Built:* 1927 *Latitude:* 43.2273 *Longitude:* -86.3368

MORRIS

Launched in 1927, USCGC Morris is now an exhibition vessel. *City:* Sacramento *State:* CA *Zip:* 95833 *Phone:* 916-715-0563 *Web:* libertymaritime.com *Email:* liberty-maritime@msn.com *Visitors welcome?* Yes *Hours:* Contact attraction directly *Admission:* Contact attraction directly *Operated by:* Liberty Maritime Museum *NR?* No *NHL?* No *Built:* 1968 *Latitude:* 38.6051 *Longitude:* -121.5240

SNOHOMISH

Launched in 1943, the Coast Guard tug Snohomish is undergoing restoration. *City:* Charleston *State:* SC *Visitors welcome?* Yes *Hours:* Contact attraction directly *Admission:* Contact attraction directly *Operated by:* Private owner *NR?* No *NHL?* No *Built:* 1943 *Latitude:* 32.7766 *Longitude:* -79.9309

SUNDEW

Launched in 1944, the buoy tender USCGC Sundew is now a floating exhibit. *Address:* 353 Harbor Drive *City:* Duluth *State:* MN *Zip:* 55802 *Phone:* 218-740-3474 *Web:* glaquarium.org *Email:* info@glaquarium.org *Visitors welcome?* Yes *Hours:* Daily, 10 a.m. to 6 p.m. *Admission:* $15 adults, $14 seniors, $12 children, two and under FREE *Operated by:* Private owners *NR?* No *NHL?* No *Built:* 1944 *Latitude:* 46.7837 *Longitude:* -92.0983

TANEY

The USCGC Taney is the only warship still afloat that saw action during the December 7, 1941 attack on Pearl Harbor. *Address:* Pier 1, Baltimore Inner Harbor (301 E. Pratt St.) *City:* Baltimore *State:* MD *Zip:* 21202 *Phone:* 410-539-1797 *Web:* www.historicships.org *Email:* administration@historicships.org *Visitors welcome?* Yes *Hours:* Contact attraction directly *Admission:* $15 adults, $13 seniors/students, $7 children six to 14, children five and under FREE *Operated by:* Historic Ships in Baltimore **NR? Yes NHL? Yes** *Built:* 1936 *Latitude:* 39.2866 *Longitude:* -76.6087

WAKEROBIN

Launched in 1926, the lighthouse tender USCGC Wakerobin is a recreational vessel. *Address:* 212 Greenup St. *City:* Covington *State:* KY *Zip:* 41011 *Phone:* 606-261-4212 *Visitors welcome?* Yes *Hours:* Contact attraction directly *Admission:* Contact attraction directly *Operated by:* Bensons, Inc. *NR?* No *NHL?* No *Built:* 1926 *Latitude:* 39.0893 *Longitude:* -84.5082

Lightships

LIGHTSHIP AMBROSE (LV-87)

A lightship designated Ambrose has served as the main beacon marking Ambrose Channel, the main shipping channel for New York Harbor from 1823 to 1967. Several ships served as the lightship, and the last, WLV 613, was commissioned in 1952. *Address:* 12 Fulton St. *City:* New York *State:* NY *Zip:* 10038 *Phone:* 212-748-8600 *Web:* www.southstreetseaportmuseum.org *Email:* info@southstseaport.org *Visitors welcome?* Yes *Hours:* Contact attraction directly *Admission:* Contact attraction directly *Operated by:* South Street Seaport Museum **NR? Yes NHL? Yes** *Built:* 1907 *Latitude:* 40.7066 *Longitude:* -74.0034

LIGHTSHIP BARNEGAT (LV 79/WAL 506)

Commissioned in 1904, the Lightship Barnegat (LV 79/WAL 506)'s station was off the Barnegat Lighthouse. The ship was decommissioned in 1967, and it has passed through the hands of several owners. It is now awaiting restoration. *Address:* Pyne Point Park *City:* Camden *State:* NJ *Visitors welcome?* Yes *Hours:* Grounds only *Admission:* Contact attraction directly *Operated by:* Barnegat Light Historical Society *NR?* No *NHL?* No *Built:* 1904 *Latitude:* 39.9263

Longitude: -75.1148

LIGHTSHIP CHESAPEAKE (LV 116)

U.S. Lightship 116 Chesapeake marked the mouth of the Chesapeake Bay for more than 29 years. From 1965-1970, Lightship 116 finished her career marking the Delaware Bay approaches. *Address:* Pier 3, Baltimore Inner Harbor (301 E. Pratt St.) *City:* Baltimore *State:* MD *Zip:* 21202 *Phone:* 410-539-1797 *Web:* www.historicships.org *Email:* administration@historicships.org *Visitors welcome?* Yes *Hours:* Contact attraction directly *Admission:* $15 adults, $13 seniors/students, $7 children six to 14, children five and under FREE *Operated by:* Historic Ships in Baltimore **NR? Yes NHL? Yes** *Built:* 1930 *Latitude:* 39.2866 *Longitude:* -76.6087

LIGHTSHIP COLUMBIA (WLV 604)

Built in 1950 in Boothbay, Maine, Lightship Columbia (WLV 604) served as the lightship marking the entrance to the Columbia River and its treacherous bar. Decommissioned in 1979, the lightship now welcomes visitors at the Columbia River Maritime Museum. *Address:* 1792 Marine Drive *City:* Astoria *State:* OR *Zip:* 97103 *Phone:* 503-325-2323 *Web:* www.crmm.org *Email:* admin@crmm.org *Visitors welcome?* Yes *Hours:* Daily, 9:30 a.m. to 5:00 p.m. *Admission:* $16 adults, $13 seniors, $5 children six to 17, children five and under FREE *Operated by:* Columbia River Maritime Museum **NR? Yes NHL? Yes** *Built:* 1950 *Latitude:* 46.1893 *Longitude:* -123.8230

LIGHTSHIP FRYING PAN SHOALS (LV-115)

Built in 1929, Lightship Frying Pan Shoals (LV-115) guarded Frying Pan Shoals, 30 miles off of Cape Fear, North Carolina, from 1930 to 1965. She is 133 feet and 3 inches in length with a 30 foot beam and she is 632 gross tons. *Address:* Pier 66 Maritime *City:* New York *State:* NY *Phone:* 212-989-6363 *Web:* www.fryingpan.com *Email:* info@pier66maritime.com *Visitors welcome?* Yes *Hours:* Daily, 11:30 a.m. to sunset *Admission:* Contact attraction directly *Operated by:* Lightship Frying Pan **NR? Yes** NHL? No *Built:* 1929 *Latitude:* 40.7143 *Longitude:* -74.0060

LIGHTSHIP HURON (LV-103)

Buit in 1920, Lightship Huron (LV-103) is now a museum ship in Port Huron, Mich. *Address:* 800 Prospect Place *City:* Port Huron *State:* MI *Zip:* 48060 *Phone:* 810-984-9768 *Web:* www.phmuseum.org *Email:* lightship@phmuseum.org *Visitors welcome?* Yes *Hours:* Contact attraction directly *Admission:* $10 adults, $7 seniors/students *Operated by:* Port Huron Museum **NR? Yes NHL? Yes** *Built:* 1921 *Latitude:* 42.9882 *Longitude:* -82.4275

LIGHTSHIP LIBERTY (LV-107)

Built in 1923 at the Bath Iron Works in Bath, Maine, Lightship Liberty (LV-107) first served at Cape Lookout Shoals, North Carolina, from 1924 to 1933. Its next station was Winter Quarter Shoals on Chesapeake Bay, where it marked the entrance until 1960. *Address:* 80 Audrey Zapp Drive *City:* Jersey City *State:* NJ *Zip:* 7304 *Phone:* 201-985-8000 *Email:* info@libertylandingmarina.com *Visitors welcome?* Yes *Hours:* Contact attraction directly *Admission:* Contact attraction directly *Operated by:* Liberty Landing Marina *NR?* No *NHL?* No *Built:* 1923 *Latitude:* 40.7094 *Longitude:* -74.0478

LIGHTSHIP NANTUCKET (LV-112)

Built in 1936, Lightship Nantucket is now a museum ship. *City:* Boston *State:* MA *Web:* nantucketlightshiplv-112.org *Email:* rmmjr2@comcast.net *Visitors welcome?* No *Operated by:* National Lighthouse Museum *NR?* No *NHL?* No *Built:* 1936 *Latitude:* 40.8168 *Longitude:* -73.0662

LIGHTSHIP NANTUCKET (WLV-612)

Built in Curtis Bay, Maryland, Lightship Nantucket (WLV-612) was one of the last lightships built by the Coast Guard. It is now a private vessel available for charter. *Address:* Nantucket Harbor *City:* Boston *State:* MA *Phone:* 617-821-6771 *Web:* www.nantucketlightship.com *Email:* info@nantucketlightship.com *Visitors welcome?* Yes *Hours:* Contact attraction directly *Admission:* Contact attraction directly *Operated by:* Nantucket Lightship WLV-612 *NR?* No *NHL?* No *Built:* 1950 *Latitude:* 41.3043 *Longitude:* -70.0453

LIGHTSHIP NANTUCKET II (WLV-613)

The Lightship Nantucket II (WLV-613) was built in 1952 and originally stationed at Ambrose Channel in New York until 1967. In 1979, it was stationed off Nantucket Island. *City:* New Bedford *State:* MA *Visitors welcome?* No *Operated by:* Private owner *NR?* No *NHL?* No *Built:* 1952 *Latitude:* 41.7626 *Longitude:* -70.6762

LIGHTSHIP OVERFALLS (LV-118)

The Lightship Overfalls (LV 118) was one of the last lightships built by the U.S. government. Commissioned in 1938, LV 118 served off Connecticut and Massachusetts between 1938 and 1972. *Address:* 219 Pilottown Road *City:* Lewes *State:* DE *Phone:* 302-644-8050 *Web:* www.overfalls.org *Visitors welcome?* Yes *Hours:* Contact attraction directly *Admission:* Contact attraction directly *Operated by:* Overfalls Maritime Museum Foundation **NR? Yes** *NHL?* No *Built:* 1938 *Latitude:* 38.7823 *Longitude:* -75.1550

LIGHTSHIP PORTSMOUTH (LV-101)

Built in 1915, the Plymouth Lightship, also known as the Cape Charles Lightship, served at several stations until she was retired in 1964. The ship is now a land-based museum. *Address:* Corner London & Water Streets *City:* Portsmouth *State:* VA *Zip:* 23704 *Phone:* 757-393-8591 *Web:* portsmouthnavalshipyardmuseum.com *Email:* navalmuseums@portsmouthva.gov *Visitors welcome?* Yes *Hours:* Fridays and Saturdays, 10 a.m. to 5 p.m., Sundays, 1 p.m. to 5 p.m. *Admission:* $2 adults/children *Operated by:* Lightship Portsmouth Museum **NR? Yes NHL? Yes** *Built:* 1915 *Latitude:* 36.8355 *Longitude:* -76.2969

LIGHTSHIP RELIEF (WLV-605)

Lightship Relief (WLV-605), one of six lightships constructed for the Coast Guard, was built by Rice Brothers Shipyard in Boothbay, Maine, in 1950. *Address:* Jack London Square *City:* Oakland *State:* CA *Zip:* 94607 *Phone:* 510-272-0544 *Visitors welcome?* Yes *Hours:* Contact attraction directly *Admission:* Contact attraction directly *Operated by:* United States Lighthouse Society **NR? Yes NHL? Yes** *Built:* 1950 *Latitude:* 37.7942 *Longitude:* -122.2760

LIGHTSHIP SWIFTSURE (LV-83)

Launched in 1904, Lightship Swiftsure (LV-83) is a floating exhibit in Seattle. *Address:* 860 Terry Ave. N. *City:* Seattle *State:* WA *Zip:* 0 *Phone:* 206-447-9800 *Web:* www.nwseaport.org *Email:* info@nwseaport.org *Visitors welcome?* Yes *Hours:* Contact attraction directly *Admission:* Donation *Operated by:* Northwest Seaport Maritime Heritage Ctr *NR?* No **NHL? Yes** *Built:* 1904 *Latitude:* 47.6276 *Longitude:* -122.3370

LIGHTSHIP UMATILLA (LV 196)

The Lightship Umatilla (LV 196) was the fourth vessel to mark Umatilla Reef off Washington State's coast. Retired in 1971, the Coast Guard decommissioned her, and it is now owned by a Ketchikan businessman. *Address:* Lewis Reef *City:* Ketchikan *State:* AK *Visitors welcome?* No *Operated by:* Southeast Stevedoring *NR?* No *NHL?* No *Latitude:* 55.3750 *Longitude:* -131.7380

LILAC

Launched in 1933, the lighthouse tender USCGC Lilac is a floating exhibit on New York's waterfront. *Address:* Pier 40 *City:* New York *State:* NY *Zip:* 10013 *Phone:* 845-612-1950 *Web:* lilacpreservationproject.org *Email:* mary@lilacpreservationproject.org *Visitors welcome?* Yes *Hours:* Saturdays and Sundays, 2 p.m. to 6 p.m. *Admission:* Contact attraction directly *Operated by:* Lilac Preservation Project *NR?* No **NHL? Yes** *Built:* 1933 *Latitude:* 40.7295 *Longitude:* -74.0127

PRESSED FOR TIME? FYDDEYE RECOMMENDS	
Sundew	Well-preserved buoy tender
Ingham	Key role in coast law enforcement
Any lightship	Unique history and stories

5

TUGBOATS & TOWBOATS

The tug Arthur Foss at South Lake Union Park in Seattle. She is currently undergoing restoration. (Photo: Joe Follansbee)

Few boats are as romantic as the tugboat, which comes in all shapes and sizes, mostly serving in ports large and small. The tugboat's cousin, the towboat, is a fixture on freshwater routes, especially the Mississippi River.

ARTHUR FOSS

Launched in 1889, the tug Arthur Foss is a floating museum and exhibit in Seattle. *Address:* 860 Terry Ave. N. *City:* Seattle *State:* WA *Zip:* 98109 *Phone:* 206-447-9800 *Web:* www.nwseaport.org *Email:*

info@nwseaport.org *Visitors welcome?* Yes *Hours:* Contact attraction directly *Admission:* Donation *Operated by:* Northwest Seaport Maritime Heritage Ctr *NR?* No **NHL?** **Yes** *Built:* 1889 *Latitude:* 47.6276 *Longitude:* -122.3370

BALTIMORE

Launched in 1906, the steam tug Baltimore is an operational museum ship. *Address:* 1415 Key Highway *City:* Baltimore *State:* MD *Zip:* 21230 *Phone:* 410-727-4808 *Web:* thebmi.org *Email:* info@thebmi.org *Visitors welcome?* Yes *Hours:* Tuesday to Sunday, 10 a.m. to 4 p.m. *Admission:* $12 adults, $9 seniors, $7 students and youth, six and under FREE *Operated by:* Baltimore Museum of Industry **NR?** **Yes** **NHL?** **Yes** *Built:* 1906 *Latitude:* 39.2742 *Longitude:* -76.6012

BARBARA H

Launched in 1923, the sternwheeler towboat Barbara H., formerly Donald B., is a floating exhibit and excursion vessel on the Ohio River. To visit, please call for an appointment. *Address:* Ohio River Mile 546 *City:* Lamb *State:* IN *Phone:* 812-427-9480 *Visitors welcome?* Yes *Hours:* Contact attraction directly *Admission:* Contact attraction directly *Operated by:* Historic Sternwheeler Preservation Society **NR?** **Yes NHL?** **Yes** *Built:* 1923 *Latitude:* 38.6920 *Longitude:* -85.1880

BUFFALO

Launched in 1923, the steam tug Buffalo is now undergoing restoration. *City:* Waterford *State:* NY *Zip:* 12188 *Phone:* 518-237-3139 *Visitors welcome?* Yes *Hours:* Contact attraction directly *Admission:* Contact attraction directly *Operated by:* Waterford Maritime Historical Society *NR?* No *NHL?* No *Built:* 1923 *Latitude:* 42.7926 *Longitude:* -73.6812

C.L. CHURCHILL

The tug C.L. Churchill, built in 1964, assists operations of the Lake Champlain Maritime Museum's schooner Lois McClure. The tug is based in Burlington. *Address:* 4472 Basin Harbor Rd. *City:* Vergennes *State:* VT *Zip:* 05491 *Phone:* 802-475-2022 *Web:* www.lcmm.org *Email:* info@lcmm.org *Visitors welcome?* Yes *Hours:* Contact attraction directly *Admission:* Contact attraction directly *Operated by:* Lake

Champlain Maritime Museum *NR?* No *NHL?* No *Built:* 1964 *Latitude:* 44.1973 *Longitude:* -73.3567

CHANCELLOR

Launched in 1938, the tug Chancellor is a floating museum under the care of the Waterford Maritime Historical Society. *Address:* 300 Greenkill Ave. *City:* Kingston *State:* NY *Zip:* 12401 *Phone:* 518-237-3139 *Visitors welcome?* Yes *Hours:* Contact attraction directly *Admission:* Contact attraction directly *Operated by:* Waterford Maritime Historical Society **NR? Yes** *NHL?* No *Built:* 1938 *Latitude:* 41.9230 *Longitude:* -74.0155

CHARLEY BORDER

The towboat Charley Border is a floating exhibit at the Arkansas River Historical Society Museum. *Address:* 5350 Cimarron Road *City:* Catoosa *State:* OK *Zip:* 74015 *Phone:* 918-266-2291 *Web:* www.tulsaports.com *Email:* info@tulsaport.com *Visitors welcome?* Yes *Hours:* Monday to Friday, 8:30 a.m. to 4:30 p.m. *Admission:* FREE *Operated by:* Arkansas River Historical Society *NR?* No *NHL?* No *Built:* 1971 *Latitude:* 36.2312 *Longitude:* -95.7417

CHARLOTTE

Launched in 1880, the tug Charlotte is a dry-berth exhibit. *Address:* 86 West Ave. *City:* West Sayville *State:* NY *Zip:* 11796 *Phone:* 631-854-4974 *Web:* www.limaritime.org *Email:* limm@limaritime.org *Visitors welcome?* Yes *Hours:* Monday to Saturday: 10 a.m. to 4 p.m.; Sunday, noon to 4 p.m. *Admission:* $4 adults, $2 senior/child three to 17, under three FREE *Operated by:* Long Island Maritime Museum *NR?* No *NHL?* No *Built:* 1880 *Latitude:* 40.7218 *Longitude:* -73.0938

DEKAURY

Launched in 1943, the tug DeKaury is undergoing restoration on San Francisco Bay. *City:* San Francisco *State:* CA *Phone:* 415-559-0217 *Email:* dekaury@gmail.com *Visitors welcome?* Yes *Hours:* Contact attraction directly *Admission:* Contact attraction directly *Operated by:* Dekaury Restoration Corporation *NR?* No *NHL?* No *Built:* 1943 *Latitude:* 37.7749 *Longitude:* -122.4190

DELAWARE

The tugboat Delaware is a product of area boatbuilding at the beginning of the 19th century. *Address:* 213 N. Talbot Street *City:* St. Michaels *State:* MD *Zip:* 21663 *Phone:* 410-745-2916 *Web:* www.cbmm.org *Email:* cbland@cbmm.org *Visitors welcome?* Yes *Hours:* Daily, hours vary by season *Admission:* $16 adults; $13 seniors over 62, students; $12 retired military; $6 kids 6 to 17; active military, kids under 6 FREE *Operated by:* Chesapeake Bay Maritime Museum *NR?* No *NHL?* No *Built:* 1912 *Latitude:* 38.7876 *Longitude:* -76.2249

DOMINION

The tug Dominion is one of 61 Miki-class tugboats commissioned by the US Army during World War II. *Address:* 400 Washington Avenue #311 *City:* Bremerton *State:* WA *Zip:* 98337 *Phone:* 206-276-1837 *Web:* www.dominiontug.org *Email:* team@dominiontug.org *Visitors welcome?* Yes *Hours:* Contact attraction directly *Admission:* Contact attraction directly *NR?* No *NHL?* No *Built:* 1944 *Latitude:* 47.5631 *Longitude:* -122.6259

EDNA G

Launched in 1896, the tug Edna G. is a floating exhibit in Two Harbors, Minn. *Address:* 522 First Ave. *City:* Two Harbors *State:* MN *Zip:* 55616 *Phone:* 218-595-0184 *Web:* friendsofednag.org *Email:* friendsoftheednag@gmail.com *Visitors welcome?* Yes *Hours:* Contact attraction directly *Admission:* Contact attraction directly *Operated by:* Friends of the Edna G **NR? Yes** *NHL?* No *Built:* 1896 *Latitude:* 47.0198 *Longitude:* -91.6696

ELISE ANN CONNORS

Launched in 1881, the tug Elise Ann Connors is privately owned. *Address:* PO Box 1065 *City:* Port Ewen *State:* NY *Zip:* 12466 *Phone:* 914-339-1052 *Visitors welcome?* No *Operated by:* Private owner *NR?* No *NHL?* No *Built:* 1881 *Latitude:* 41.9105 *Longitude:* -73.9845

ELIZABETH LEA

Launched in 1939, the towboat Elizabeth Lea is a private vessel that visits local festivals and showcases the importance of inland waterways. *Address:* Lighthouse Point Yacht Club *City:* Aurora *State:*

IN *Zip:* 47001 *Phone:* 513-373-0750 Visitors welcome: Yes *Hours:* Contract attraction directly *Admission:* Contact attraction directly *Operated by:* Private owner *NR?* No *NHL?* No *Built:* 1939 *Latitude:* 39.0287 *Longitude:* -84.8855

EPPLETON HALL

Launched in 1914, the paddle tug Eppleton Hall is now a museum ship at the San Francisco Maritime National Historical Park. *Address:* San Francisco Maritime National Historical Park *City:* San Francisco *State:* CA *Zip:* 94123 *Phone:* 415-561-7000 *Web:* www.nps.gov/safr/ *Visitors welcome?* Yes *Hours:* Contact attraction directly *Admission:* $15 *Admission:* Contact attraction directly *Operated by:* San Francisco Maritime National Historical Park *NR?* No *NHL?* No *Built:* 1914 *Latitude:* 37.8070 *Longitude:* -122.4220

F.D. RUSSELL

Launched in 1939, the owners of the tug F.D. Russell also own and operated the Ponce de Leon Inlet Lighthouse. *Address:* 4931 South Peninsula Drive *City:* Ponce Inlet *State:* FL *Zip:* 32127 *Phone:* 386-761-1821 *Web:* www.ponceinlet.org *Visitors welcome?* Yes *Hours:* Contact attraction directly *Admission:* Contact attraction directly *Operated by:* Ponce de Leon Inlet Light Station Preservation Association *NR?* No *NHL?* No *Built:* 1938 *Latitude:* 29.0807 *Longitude:* -80.9281

FRANCES

Launched in 1957, the tug Frances is an operating tug. *Address:* 300 Greenkill Ave. *City:* Kingston *State:* NY *Zip:* 12401 *Visitors welcome?* No *Hours:* Contact attraction directly *Admission:* Contact attraction directly *Operated by:* NYS Marine Highway *NR?* No *NHL?* No *Built:* 1957 *Latitude:* 41.9230 *Longitude:* -74.0155

GEORGE M. VERITY

Launched in 1927, the river towboat George M. Verity is a dry-berth exhibit at Victory Park on the Mississippi River. *Address:* 200 Mississippi Dr. *City:* Keokuk *State:* IA *Zip:* 52632 *Phone:* 319-524-2050 *Visitors welcome?* Yes *Hours:* Memorial Day to Labor Day, daily, 9 a.m. to 5 p.m. *Admission:* $4 adults, $3 seniors, $2 children ages 8-18, children 7 and under FREE. *Operated by:* Verity Museum Commission

NR? *Yes* *NHL?* *Yes* *Built:* 1927 *Latitude:* 40.3958 *Longitude:* -91.3815

HELEN MCALLISTER

Launched in 1900, the tug Helen McAllister is a floating exhibit at the South Street Seaport Museum. *Address:* 12 Fulton St. *City:* New York *State:* NY *Zip:* 10038 *Phone:* 212-748-8600 *Web:* www.southstreetseaportmuseum.org *Email:* info@southstseaport.org *Visitors welcome?* Yes *Hours:* Contact attraction directly *Admission:* Contact attraction directly *Operated by:* South Street Seaport Museum *NR?* No *NHL?* No *Built:* 1900 *Latitude:* 40.7066 *Longitude:* -74.0034

Most historic vessels are maintained by private non-profit groups. Please consider a tax-deductible donation beyond your admission fee.

HERCULES

Launched in 1907, the steam tug Hercules is now a museum ship at the San Francisco Maritime National Historical Park. *Address:* San Francisco Maritime National Historical Park *City:* San Francisco *State:* CA *Zip:* 94123 *Phone:* 415-561-7000 *Web:* www.nps.gov/safr/ *Visitors welcome?* Yes *Hours:* Contact attraction directly *Admission:* $15 *Operated by:* San Francisco Maritime National Historical Park *NR?* *Yes* *NHL?* *Yes* *Built:* 1907 *Latitude:* 37.8070 *Longitude:* -122.4220

JOHN PURVES

Launched in 1919, the tug John Purves is an historic vessel berthed near the Door County Maritime Museum. *Address:* 120 N. Madison Ave. *City:* Sturgeon Bay *State:* WI *Zip:* 54235 *Phone:* 920-743-5958 *Web:* www.dcmm.org *Email:* info@dcmm.org *Visitors welcome?* Yes *Hours:* Wednesday, Friday, Saturday, Sunday, 11 a.m. to 3 p.m. *Admission:* $10 adults, $5 youth 5-17, children under four FREE *Operated by:* Door County Maritime Museum & Lighthouse Preservation Society *NR?* No *NHL?* No *Built:* 1919 *Latitude:* 44.8301 *Longitude:* -87.3844

JOSIAH WHITE II

The replica towboat Josiah White II is a passenger excursion vessel that is part of the National Canal Museum. *Address:* 2750 Hugh Moore Park Road *City:* Easton *State:* PA *Zip:* 18042 *Phone:* 610-923-

3458 *Web:* canals.org *Email:* loretta@delawareandlehigh.org *Visitors welcome?* Yes *Hours:* Contact attraction directly *Admission:* Contact attraction directly *Operated by:* National Canal Museum *NR?* No *NHL?* No *Latitude:* 40.6912 *Longitude:* -75.2099

JUPITER

Launched in 1902, the tug Jupiter is now an operating museum ship. *Address:* Foot of Market Street *City:* Philadelphia *State:* PA *Zip:* 19106 *Phone:* 215-238-0280 *Web:* philashipguild.org *Email:* office@philashipguild.org *Visitors welcome?* Yes *Hours:* Contact attraction directly *Admission:* Contact attraction directly *Operated by:* Philadelphia Ship Preservation Guild *NR?* No *NHL?* No *Built:* 1902 *Latitude:* 39.9505 *Longitude:* -75.1481

KINGSTON II

The harbor tug Kingston II is thought to be one of the earliest all-welded vessels. *Address:* 75 Greenmanville Avenue *City:* Mystic *State:* CT *Zip:* 06355 *Phone:* 860-572-5315 *Web:* www.mysticseaport.org *Visitors welcome?* Yes *Hours:* Thursday to Sunday, 10 a.m. to 4 p.m. *Admission:* $23.95 adults; $21.95 seniors; $19.95 youth 13-17; $16.95 child 4-12 *Operated by:* Mystic Seaport *NR?* No *NHL?* No *Built:* 1930 *Latitude:* 41.362992 *Longitude:* -71.963389

LOGSDON

Launched in 1941, the towboat Logsdon is a dry-berth exhibit at the Mississippi River Museum. *Address:* 350 East Third St. *City:* Dubuque *State:* IA *Zip:* 52001 *Phone:* 563-557-9545 *Toll-free:* 800-226-3369 *Web:* rivermuseum.com *Visitors welcome?* Yes *Hours:* Daily, 9 a.m. to 5 p.m. *Admission:* $19.95 adults, $17.95 seniors, $14.95 youth three to 17 *Operated by:* Dubuque County Historical Society *NR?* No *NHL?* No *Built:* 1941 *Latitude:* 42.4963 *Longitude:* -90.6591

LONE STAR

Launched in 1868, the towboat Lone Star is a dry-berth exhibit at the Buffalo Bill Museum in Le Claire. *Address:* 199 N. Front St. *City:* Le Claire *State:* IA *Zip:* 52753 *Phone:* 563-289-5580 *Web:* www.buffalobillmuseumleclaire.com *Email:* contact@buffalobillmuseumleclaire.com *Visitors welcome?* Yes *Hours:*

Monday to Friday, 10 a.m. to 4 p.m.; Saturday and Sunday, noon to 4 p.m. *Admission:* Contact attraction directly *Operated by:* Buffalo Bill Museum *NR? Yes NHL? Yes Built:* 1868 *Latitude:* 41.5976 *Longitude:* -90.3432

LUDINGTON

Launched in 1944, the tug Ludington is a floating exhibit in Kewaunee Harbor. *Address:* Port of Kewaunee *City:* Kewaunee *State:* WI *Zip:* 54216 *Phone:* 920-388-5000 *Email:* info@cityofkewaunee.org *Visitors welcome?* Yes *Hours:* Contact attraction directly *Admission:* Contact attraction directly *Operated by:* City of Kewaunee *NR?* No *NHL?* No *Built:* 1944 *Latitude:* 44.4583 *Longitude:* -87.5031

LUNA

Launched in 1930, the tugboat Luna is a museum ship undergoing restoration in the Boston area. *Address:* Commonwealth Pier *City:* Boston *State:* MA *Zip:* 02446 *Phone:* 617-282-1941 *Web:* www.tugboatluna.org *Email:* info@tugboatluna.org *Visitors welcome?* Yes *Hours:* Contact attraction directly *Admission:* Contact attraction directly *Operated by:* Luna Preservation Society *NR?* No *NHL? Yes Built:* 1930 *Latitude:* 42.3422 *Longitude:* -71.1241

MATHILDA

Launched in 1899, the tug Mathilda is a dry-berth exhibit at the Hudson River Maritime Museum. *Address:* 50 Rondout Landing *City:* Kingston *State:* NY *Zip:* 12401 *Phone:* 845-338-0071 *Web:* www.hrmm.org *Email:* info@hrmm.org *Visitors welcome?* Yes *Hours:* Contact attraction directly *Admission:* $9 adults; $6 seniors, children 4 to 18; children four and under FREE *Operated by:* Hudson River Maritime Museum *NR?* No *NHL?* No *Built:* 1899 *Latitude:* 41.9235 *Longitude:* -73.9836

MAUD

The 40-foot diesel towboat Maud is part of the collection of the Mississippi River Museum. It once operated on the Illinois River and is an example of 20th century commercial river craft. *Address:* 350 East Third St. *City:* Dubuque *State:* IA *Zip:* 52001 *Phone:* 563-557-9545 *Web:* www.rivermuseum.com *Visitors welcome?* Yes *Hours:* Daily,

9 a.m. to 5 p.m. *Admission:* $19.95 adults, $17.95 seniors, $14.95 youth three to 17 *Operated by:* Dubuque County Historical Society *NR?* No *NHL?* No *Latitude:* 42.4963 *Longitude:* -90.6591

MAZAPETA

Mazapeta is a former U.S. Navy tug/fire boat built in 1943. She is used to educate people about World War II and the importance of tugboats. *Address:* Empire Tract Road *City:* Stockton *State:* CA *Phone:* 650-483-1963 *Visitors welcome?* Yes *Hours:* Contact attraction directly *Admission:* Contact attraction directly *NR?* No *NHL?* No *Built:* 1943 *Latitude:* 37.7906 *Longitude:* -122.3260

OHIO

Launched in 1903, the fire tug Ohio is now on display on the Cleveland waterfront. *Address:* 1701 Front Street *City:* Toledo *State:* OH *Zip:* 43605 *Phone:* 419-214-5000 *Web:* nmgl.org *Email:* info@nmgl.org *Visitors welcome?* Yes *Hours:* Monday to Saturday 11 a.m. to 3:30 p.m., Sunday, noon to 3:30 p.m. *Admission:* $11 adults, $10 seniors, active military, $8 youth six to 17, children five and under FREE *Operated by:* National Museum of the Great Lakes *NR?* No *NHL?* No *Built:* 1911 *Latitude:* 41.6565 *Longitude:* -83.5152

PAUL BUNYAN

Launched in 1926, the towboat Paul Bunyan is a dry-berth exhibit. *Address:* 36094 Memory Lane *City:* Polson *State:* MT *Zip:* 59860 *Phone:* 406-883-6804 *Web:* www.miracleofamericamuseum.org *Email:* info@miracleofamericamuseum.org *Visitors welcome?* Yes *Hours:* Daily, 9 a.m. to 5 p.m. *Admission:* $10 adults, $2 children two to 12, under two FREE *Operated by:* Miracle of America Museum and Pioneer Village *NR?* No *NHL?* No *Built:* 1926 *Latitude:* 47.6791 *Longitude:* -114.1070

PORTLAND

Launched in 1947, the ship assist towboat Portland is a floating exhibit. *Address:* 115 SW Ash St. Suite 400C *City:* Portland *State:* OR *Zip:* 97204 *Phone:* 503-224-7724 *Web:* www.oregonmaritimemuseum.org *Email:* info@oregonmaritimemuseum.org *Visitors welcome?* Yes *Hours:*

Wednesday, Friday and Saturday, 11 a.m. to 4 p.m. *Admission:* $7 adults, $5 seniors, $4 students 13 to 18, $3 children six to 12, under six FREE *Operated by:* Oregon Maritime Museum **NR? Yes** *NHL?* No *Built:* 1947 *Latitude:* 45.5218 *Longitude:* -122.6720

Q.A. GILLMORE

Launched in 1913, the steam tug Q.A. Gillmore is privately owned. *Address:* Blue Star Highway and Union St. *City:* Holland *State:* MI *Zip:* 49423 *Visitors welcome?* No *Hours:* Contact attraction directly *Admission:* Contact attraction directly *Operated by:* Private owner *NR?* No *NHL?* No *Built:* 1913 *Latitude:* 42.6466 *Longitude:* -86.2025

SAND MAN

Launched in 1910, the tug Sand Man is now an operational museum ship. *Address:* Eastbay Dr NE and Olympia Ave NE *City:* Olympia *State:* WA *Phone:* 360-786-9474 *Web:* www.tugsandman.org *Email:* tugsandman@gmail.com *Visitors welcome?* Yes *Hours:* Saturday, Sunday, some holidays; 10 a.m. to 3 p.m. *Admission:* FREE *Operated by:* Sand Man Foundation **NR? Yes** *NHL?* No *Built:* 1910 *Latitude:* 47.0465 *Longitude:* -122.9030

SERGEANT FLOYD

Launched in 1932, the towboat Sergeant Floyd is a dry-berth exhibit and welcome center. *Address:* 1000 Larsen Park Road *City:* Sioux City *State:* IA *Zip:* 51103 *Phone:* 712-279-0198 *Web:* www.siouxcitymuseum.org/sgt-floyd-river-museum-a-welcome-center *Email:* scpm@sioux-city.org *Visitors welcome?* Yes *Hours:* Daily, 10 a.m. to 4 p.m. *Admission:* FREE *Operated by:* Sergeant Floyd River Museum & Welcome Center **NR? Yes NHL? Yes** *Built:* 1932 *Latitude:* 42.4879 *Longitude:* -96.4004

SPIRIT OF ALGOMA

Launched in 1916, the steam tug Spirit of Algoma is in the collection of the Northeastern Maritime Historical Foundation. *City:* Duluth *State:* MN *Visitors welcome?* Yes *Hours:* Contact attraction directly *Admission:* Contact attraction directly *Operated by:* Northeastern Maritime Historical Foundation *NR?* No *NHL?* No *Built:* 1916 *Latitude:* 46.7833 *Longitude:* -92.1066

ST. HELENA III

The towboat St. Helena III is a replica of a vessel that operated on the Ohio & Erie Canal more than a century ago. *Address:* 125 Tuscarawas St. W. *City:* Canal Fulton *State:* OH *Zip:* 44614 *Phone:* 330-854-6835 *Web:* www.discovercanalfulton.com/canalway_center.html *Email:* canalway@cityofcanalfulton-oh.gov *Visitors welcome?* Yes *Hours:* April and October: Saturday and Sunday, 10 a.m. to 4 p.m.; May to September: Daily, 10 a.m. to 6 p.m. *Admission:* Contact attraction directly *Operated by:* Canal Fulton Heritage Society *NR?* No *NHL?* No *Latitude:* 40.8892 *Longitude:* -81.5985

TAVERN

The 42-foot Tavern is a towboat/dredger tender that accompanies the steamboat William M. Black. *Address:* 350 East Third St. *City:* Dubuque *State:* IA *Zip:* 52001 *Phone:* 563-557-9545 *Web:* www.rivermuseum.com *Visitors welcome?* Yes *Hours:* Daily, 9 a.m. to 5 p.m. *Admission:* $19.95 adults, $17.95 seniors, $14.95 youth three to 17 *Operated by:* Dubuque County Historical Society *NR?* No *NHL?* No *Latitude:* 42.4963 *Longitude:* -90.6591

URGER

Launched in 1901, the tug Urger is now an educational vessel on the New York Canal System. *Address:* 200 Southern Blvd *City:* Albany *State:* NY *Zip:* 12209 *Phone:* 518-436-2799 *Web:* canals.ny.gov *Visitors welcome?* Yes *Hours:* Contact attraction directly *Admission:* Contact attraction directly *Operated by:* New York State Canals *NR?* No *NHL?* No *Built:* 1901 *Latitude:* 42.6298 *Longitude:* -73.7765

W.O. DECKER

Launched in 1930, the tug W.O. Decker is an operational museum vessel. *Address:* 12 Fulton St. *City:* New York *State:* NY *Zip:* 10038 *Phone:* 212-748-8600 *Web:* www.southstreetseaportmuseum.org *Email:* info@southstseaport.org *Visitors welcome?* Yes *Hours:* Contact attraction directly *Admission:* Contact attraction directly *Operated by:* South Street Seaport Museum *NR? Yes NHL?* No *Built:* 1930 *Latitude:* 40.7066 *Longitude:* -74.0034

W.P. SNYDER, JR.

Launched in 1918, the towboat W.P. Snyder, Jr. is the last steam-powered, stern-wheeled towboat in the United States. It is now a floating exhibit on the Muskingum River near the Ohio River Museum. *Address:* 601 Front Street *City:* Marietta *State:* OH *Zip:* 45750 *Phone:* 740-373-3750 *Web:* www.campusmartiusmuseum.org *Email:* info@campusmartiusmuseum.org *Visitors welcome?* Yes *Hours:* Monday to Saturday, 9:30 a.m. to 5 p.m., Sundays and holidays, noon to 5 p.m. *Admission:* $7 adults, $4 students, under five FREE *Operated by:* Friends of the Museums **NR? Yes NHL? Yes** *Built:* 1918 *Latitude:* 39.4210 *Longitude:* -81.4640

PRESSED FOR TIME? FYDDEYE RECOMMENDS	
Arthur Foss	A movie star in the 1930s
Eppleton Hall	Rare preserved paddle tug
Maud	Mississippi River workboat
W.O. Decker	New York maritime history

6

COMMERCIAL, EXCURSION, & RESEARCH VESSELS

The William G. Mather is a Great Lakes freighter that has been turned into a steamship museum. (Photo: Perry Quan / Wikimedia Commons)

In today's transportation world, where air travel gets all the attention, the world relies on the cargo vessel, which carries everything from food to fuel. Communities preserve these ships as a way to remember the roots of their economies. Some museums, especially those dedicated to science, preserve research vessels to show the progress of knowledge.

The Forgotten History of Steamboats on the Okanogan River

By Natalie Johnson

The rich history of steamboats on the Mississippi River often overshadows the dynamic history of steamboating on another major American river: the Columbia. Just as steamboats pushed the boundaries of the Midwest into the Mississippi's tributaries, aggressive captains took sternwheelers carrying settlers, freight and supplies up the Okanogan River, a major branch of the Columbia draining the eastern foothills of the Cascade Mountains, to expand one of the last frontiers in the United States, the Okanogan Valley.

The steamer Okanogan, photographed by pioneer photographer Frank Matsura, passes under a steel bridge at Okanogan in 1914. (Photo: Okanogan County Historical Society)

Boats like the City of Ellensburg and the Enterprise carried pioneers into a landscape marked by bone-dry coulees and populated with rattlesnakes, quail and a few hardy residents. On one side of the Okanogan River was the Colville Indian Reservation, one of the largest reservations in the country, and on the other, growing pioneer towns like Monse, Okanogan and Riverside. Settlers sought cheap farmland, logging jobs, or even the Mother Lode in one of the area's mining towns, some of which were already declining by the time sternwheelers navigated the Okanogan. The boats at times reached as far north as Oroville, barely five miles south of the Canadian border. Today, the only traces of this brief maritime history remain in the museums, ghost towns, and hidden remnants of steamboating ingenuity.

The journey wasn't easy for the early settlers. From the 1880s to the 1910's, they could take a train as far as Wenatchee, located almost dead center in Washington State beside the Columbia. But travelers needed another way to venture deep into the frontier towns of the Okanogan Valley further north. Some took a stage-coach, others walked, but most relied on riverboats, primarily steam-powered sternwheelers, that transported people, mail, and goods from one frontier town to the next.

The first sternwheeler to service the Okanogan Valley was the City of Ellensburg, which until 1893 was the only steamboat in Okanogan County. It made its first journey in July 1888 from Pasco to the Columbia River, finishing on the Okanogan River near Monse, a town that once boomed in the area between present-day Brewster, now a small town surrounded by fruit orchards near the Columbia's confluence with the Okanogan river, and the city of Okanogan.

Most of the sternwheelers braving the rapids of the Columbia and Okanogan rivers were managed by the Columbia and Okanogan (C&O) Steamboat Company. Throughout most of the year, the company's sternwheelers were lucky to make it as far as Brewster, and were often delayed in Wenatchee due to low water or bad weather. But during the spring thaw, for six to eight weeks when snowmelt from the Cascades swelled the river, riverboats could make it past Brewster to make stops in Okanogan, Omak, Riverside, and very rarely, past McLoughlin Falls to Oroville.

At first glance, the sternwheelers of the Okanogan look much like their more famous cousins on the Mississippi. But the Okanogan craft had several key differences which helped make them functional in the river's shallow waters. One of the largest sternwheelers was the Okanogan. At 137 feet long, the craft was less than half the size of the second largest Mississippi riverboat, the Mississippi Queen. The

Columbia and Okanogan sternwheelers also had a much shallower draft than the larger boats on the Mississippi, only requiring two feet of water.

Over time, boat builders adapted classic designs to the demands of the Okanogan and rapids at Entiat and Pateros on the Columbia. One small sternwheeler, the Enterprise, built in 1905, had only a seven-inch draft.

While the sternwheelers' steam engines, fueled by wood cut from surrounding forest land, could propel them through calm water easily, crews developed creative ways to haul the riverboats over the rapids at Entiat and Pateros, which was called Ives Landing until 1900. To get past these natural barriers, crews scrambled ashore and attached tow cables to hooks fastened to rocks. Crews engaged a forward deck winch to tighten the cables and pull the boat up and over the rapids. There are also accounts of crew members standing on the shore and using ropes to re-orient a sternwheeler stuck on a rock. Though the Pateros Rapids have been long covered by overflow from the Wells Hydroelectric Dam, built in 1967, some of the cable hooks can still be viewed near the former site of the rapids.

As on other major rivers in the United States, sternwheelers encouraged the growth of the Okanogan Valley; four separate towns were founded for the express purpose of creating more steamboat landings near the mouth of the Okanogan River. Three of these settlements, Port Columbia, Swansea, and Virginia City, don't exist today. Brewster, founded on a pioneer's homestead, is now a hub of apple orchards and fruit packing plants. The riverboat traffic also shaped the built landscape. In Okanogan, engineers erected high bridges over the river for pedestrians. The Okanogan high bridge is immortalized on a downtown building in modern Okanogan. in a mural based on a famous photograph by one of the Okanogan Valley's most famous settlers, Frank Matsura. The photographer also took many images of the visiting steamboats.

Though the Mississippi River's steamboats lasted more than a century as major modes of transportation, the sternwheelers of the upper Columbia River and Okanogan River barely lasted a generation. In 1914, the Great Northern Railroad reached Oroville from Wenatchee, making the Okanogan sternwheelers obsolete with reliable and efficient rail service twice daily.

Over the next few years, most of the sternwheelers were allowed to disintegrate, sink, or burn. Some of the towns they helped populate fared no better. Monse is little more than a ghost town today, with only a few homes, and the empty shells of its schoolhouse, general store and post office. Riverside, a once booming steamboat stop on the Okanogan, now only has a small general store and a few hundred residents.

A "u-bolt" used to haul steamboats over Okanogan River rapids is one of the few physical reminders of the river's steamboat history. (Photo: Okanogan County Historical Society)

The cities of Pateros, Brewster, Okanogan, Omak, Tonasket, and Oroville still have populations in the thousands, supported by the region's agriculture economy, but most traces of the sternwheeler's legacy have been lost. The Okanogan County Historical Society has done extensive research on the history of sternwheelers in Okanogan County, and has a large collection of historical photos and documents.

However, most physical evidence of the brief life of Okanogan and upper Columbia River steamboats, and the part they played in bringing thousands of settlers into the Okanogan Valley, is gone. But if you visit towns like Pateros, Okanogan or Oroville, and experience the rolling rivers and majestically barren landscape, untouched even in the industrial world we live in, you may be able to imagine why pioneers made the arduous journey into the frontier on the sternwheelers of the Okanogan Valley.

Natalie Johnson was born in Seattle, but grew up in Okanogan, Wash. She is an award-winning journalist who is now managing editor of the Methow Valley News.

Cargo Carriers

COL. JAMES M. SCHOONMAKER
Launched in 1911, the Great Lakes freighter Col. James M. Schoonmaker is now a museum ship. *Address:* 1701 Front Street *City:* Toledo *State:* OH *Zip:* 43605 *Phone:* 419-214-5000 *Web:* nmgl.org *Email:* info@nmgl.org *Visitors welcome?* Yes *Hours:* Monday to Saturday 10 a.m. to 5 p.m., Sunday, noon to 5 p.m. *Admission:* $11 adults, $10 seniors, active military, $8 youth six to 17, children five and under FREE *Operated by:* National Museum of the Great Lakes *NR?* No *NHL?* No *Built:* 1911 *Latitude:* 41.6565 *Longitude:* -83.5152

DAY PECKINPAUGH
Launched in 1921, the motor ship Day Peckinpaugh is a traveling exhibit and classroom managed by the New York State Museum. *Address:* 222 Madison Ave. *City:* Albany *State:* NY *Zip:* 12230 *Phone:* 518-474-5877 *Web:* www.nysm.nysed.gov *Visitors welcome?* Yes *Hours:* Contact attraction directly for reservations *Operated by:* New York State Museum *NR?* No *NHL?* No *Built:* 1921 *Latitude:* 42.6481 *Longitude:* -73.7600

MADAKET
Launched in 1910, the launch Madaket is operated as an excursion vessel by the Humboldt Bay Maritime Museum. *Address:* Foot of F Street *City:* Eureka *State:* CA *Zip:* 95501 *Phone:* 707-444-9440 *Web:* www.humboldtbaymaritimemuseum.com *Visitors welcome?* Yes *Hours:* Contact attraction directly *Operated by:* Humboldt Bay Maritime Museum *NR?* No *NHL?* No *Built:* 1910 *Latitude:* 40.7933 *Longitude:* -

124.1640

MARION M

Launched in 1932, the chandlery lighter Marion M. is a floating exhibit at the South Street Seaport Museum. *Address:* 12 Fulton St. *City:* New York *State:* NY *Zip:* 10038 *Phone:* 212-748-8600 *Web:* www.southstreetseaportmuseum.org *Email:* info@southstseaport.org *Visitors welcome?* Yes *Hours:* Contact attraction directly *Admission:* Contact attraction directly *Operated by:* South Street Seaport Museum *NR?* No *NHL?* No *Built:* 1932 *Latitude:* 40.7066 *Longitude:* -74.0034

MARY WHALEN

Launched in 1938, the tanker Mary Whalen is a floating museum in Brooklyn, New York. *Address:* Pier 11 *City:* Brooklyn *State:* NY *Phone:* 917-414-0565 *Web:* www.portsidenewyork.org *Email:* chiclet@portsidenewyork.org *Visitors welcome?* Yes *Hours:* Contact attraction directly *Operated by:* Portside New York *NR?* No *NHL?* No *Built:* 1938 *Latitude:* 40.7729 *Longitude:* -73.9954

METEOR

Launched in 1896, the whaleback Meteor is a dry-berth exhibit on the Superior waterfront. *Address:* 200 Marina Dr. *City:* Superior *State:* WI *Zip:* 54880 *Phone:* 715-394-5712 *Web:* www.superiorpublicmuseums.org *Email:* info@superiorpublicmuseums.org *Visitors welcome?* Yes *Hours:* Contact attraction directly *Admission:* $5 adults and children, under five FREE *Operated by:* Superior Public Museums **NR? Yes** *NHL?* No *Built:* 1896 *Latitude:* 46.7213 *Longitude:* -92.0653

SAVANNAH

The Savannah is a one-of-a-kind nuclear-powered cargo vessel now undergoing preservation and decommissioning in Baltimore. *Address:* 4601 Newgate Avenue *City:* Baltimore *State:* MD *Zip:* 21224 *Phone:* 202-680-2066 *Web:* ns-savannah.org *Visitors welcome?* No *Hours:* Contact attraction directly *Admission:* Contact attraction directly *NR?* No *NHL?* No Operated by N.S. Savannah Association *Latitude:* 39.2605 *Longitude:* -76.5577

VALLEY CAMP

Launched in 1917, the Great Lake freighter Valley Camp is now a museum ship. *Address:* 501 East Water Street *City:* Sault Ste. Marie *State:* MI *Zip:* 49783 *Phone:* 906-632-3658 *Web:* www.saulthistoricsites.com/museum-ship-valley-camp *Visitors welcome?* Yes *Hours:* Contact attraction directly *Admission:* Contact attraction directly *Operated by:* Sault Historic Sites **NR? Yes** *NHL?* No *Built:* 1917 *Latitude:* 46.4987 *Longitude:* -84.3374

WELCOME (MILK BOAT)

Launched in 1919, the milk boat Welcome is undergoing restoration. *Address:* 1220 Sherman Ave. *City:* North Bend *State:* OR *Zip:* 97459 *Phone:* 541-756-6320 *Web:* www.cooshistory.org *Email:* info@cooshistory.org *Visitors welcome?* Yes *Hours:* Contact attraction directly *Admission:* $7 adults, $3 children 5-17, under five FREE *Operated by:* Coos History Museum *NR?* No *NHL?* No *Built:* 1919 *Latitude:* 43.3966 *Longitude:* -124.2240

WILLIAM A. IRVIN

Launched in 1938, the Great Lakes freighter William A. Irvin is now a floating exhibit. *Address:* 350 Harbor Drive *City:* Duluth *State:* MN *Zip:* 55802 *Phone:* 218-722-7876 *Web:* www.decc.org/attractions/irvin/ *Visitors welcome?* Yes *Hours:* Friday to Sunday, 10 a.m. to 5 p.m. Admision: $15 adults; $10 students, seniors, active military; children 10 and under FREE *Operated by:* Duluth Entertainment Convention Center **NR? Yes** *NHL?* No *Built:* 1938 *Latitude:* 46.7837 *Longitude:* -92.0983

WILLIAM G. MATHER

Launched in 1925, the Great Lakes freighter William G. Mather is now a museum ship. *Address:* 305 Mather Way *City:* Cleveland *State:* OH *Zip:* 44114 *Phone:* 216-574-6262 *Web:* wgmather.nhlink.net *Visitors welcome?* Yes *Hours:* Monday to Saturday, 10 a.m. to 5 p.m., Sunday, Noon to 5 p.m. *Admission:* Contact attraction directly *Operated by:* Great Lakes Science Center *NR?* No *NHL?* No *Built:* 1925 *Latitude:* 41.5594 *Longitude:* -81.5989

Ferries

ADIRONDACK

Launched in 1913, the Adirondack is an operating car and passenger ferry on Lake Champlain. *Address:* 1 King Street Dock *City:* Burlington *State:* VT *Zip:* 05401 *Phone:* 802-864-9804 *Web:* www.ferries.com *Email:* customerservice@ferries.com *Visitors welcome?* Yes *Hours:* Contact attraction directly *Admission:* Contact attraction directly *Operated by:* Lake Champlain Transportation Company *NR?* No *NHL?* No *Built:* 1913 *Latitude:* 44.4745 *Longitude:* -73.2202

BADGER

Launched in 1952, the car ferry Badger is still in operation on Lake Michigan. *Address:* 701 Maritime Drive *City:* Ludington *State:* MI *Zip:* 49431 *Phone:* 231-843-1509 Toll-free: 800-841-4243 *Web:* www.ssbadger.com *Email:* info@ssbadger.com *Visitors welcome?* Yes *Hours:* Contact attraction directly *Admission:* Contact attraction directly *Operated by:* Lake Michigan Car Ferry Service **NR? Yes** *NHL?* No *Built:* 1952 *Latitude:* 43.9494 *Longitude:* -86.4498

BEMUS POINT-STOW FERRY

The Bemus Point-Stow Ferry is one of the last remaining cable-drawn ferries in the nation. *Address:* Stow Ferry Road *City:* Stow *State:* NY *Zip:* 14710 *Phone:* 716-326-6633 *Web:* bemuspointstowferry.org *Email:* bemuspointstowferry@gmail.com *Visitors welcome?* Yes *Hours:* Memorial Day to Labor Day: Fridays, 5 p.m. to 9 p.m.; Saturday and Sunday, noon to 9 p.m. *Admission:* Donation *Operated by:* Sea Lion Project, Ltd *NR?* No *NHL?* No *Latitude:* 42.1561 *Longitude:* -79.4030

BERKELEY

Launched in 1898, the steam ferry Berkeley operated for 60 years on San Francisco Bay and is now on exhibit at the San Diego Maritime Museum. *Address:* 1492 North Harbor Drive *City:* San Diego *State:* CA *Zip:* 92101 *Phone:* 619-234-9153 *Web:* www.sdmaritime.com *Email:* support@sdmaritime.org *Visitors welcome?* Yes *Hours:* Daily, 10 a.m. to 8 p.m. *Admission:* $20 18+; $15 seniors, military, students; $10 children three to 12; children under two FREE *Operated by:* Maritime Museum Association of San Diego **NR? Yes NHL? Yes** *Built:* 1898 *Latitude:* 32.7276 *Longitude:* -117.1800

CARLISLE II

Carlisle II is an historic mosquito fleet vessel, one of hundreds of small passenger vessels that ferried passengers to dozens of small towns and cities before the advent of good roads and car ferries. *Address:* 10 Washington Avenue *City:* Bremerton *State:* WA *Visitors welcome?* Yes *Hours:* Daily *Admission:* Contact attraction directly *Operated by:* Kitsap Transit *NR?* No *NHL?* No *Built:* 1917 *Latitude:* 47.5673 *Longitude:* -122.6240

CITY OF MILWAUKEE

Launched in 1931, the railroad car ferry City of Milwaukee is now a floating museum. *Address:* 99 Arthur Street *City:* Manistee *State:* MI *Zip:* 49660 *Phone:* 231-723-3587 *Web:* www.carferry.com *Email:* sscityofmilwaukee@gmail.com *Visitors welcome?* Yes *Hours:* Contact attraction directly *Admission:* $10 adults, $8 seniors, children six to 17, children under six FREE *Operated by:* S.S. City of Milwaukee - National Historic Landmark **NR? Yes NHL? Yes** *Built:* 1931 *Latitude:* 44.2595 *Longitude:* -86.3164

COMMANDER

Launched in 1917, the Commander is a former operating passenger ferry. *Address:* 616 Beach Road *City:* West Haverstraw *State:* NY *Zip:* 10993 *Phone:* 845-534-7245 *Visitors welcome?* No *Hours:* None *Admission:* Contact attraction directly *Operated by:* Unknown; listed for sale in 2020. **NR? Yes** *NHL?* No *Built:* 1917 *Latitude:* 41.2125 *Longitude:* -73.9689

EUREKA

Launched in 1890, the current configuration of the Eureka is as a passenger and car ferry. It is now a museum ship at the San Francisco Maritime National Historical Park. *Address:* San Francisco Maritime National Historical Park *City:* San Francisco *State:* CA *Zip:* 94123 *Phone:* 415-561-7000 *Web:* www.nps.gov/safr/ *Visitors welcome?* Yes *Hours:* 8 a.m. to 5 p.m. *Admission:* $15 *Operated by:* San Francisco

Maritime National Historical Park *NR?* *Yes* *NHL?* *Yes* *Built:* 1890
Latitude: 37.8070 *Longitude:* -122.4220

GENERAL HARRISON

The passenger vessel General Harrison is a mule-drawn replica of
canal boats used on the Miami & Erie Canal. *Address:* 9845 North
Hardin Road *City:* Piqua *State:* OH *Zip:* 45356 *Phone:* 937-773-2522
Web: touringohio.com/southwest/miami/piqua/piqua-historic-
area.html *Visitors welcome?* Yes *Hours:* Contact attraction directly
Admission: Contact attraction directly *Operated by:* Piqua Historical
Area *NR?* No *NHL?* No *Latitude:* 40.1810 *Longitude:* -84.2559

KIRKLAND

Lauched in 1934, the car ferry Kirkland is now an excursion vessel. It
is currently undergoing restoration in Astoria, Ore. *City:* Astoria *State:*
OR *Visitors welcome?* No *Operated by:* Argosy Cruises *NR?* *Yes* *NHL?*
No *Built:* 1934 *Latitude:* 47.6765 *Longitude:* -122.2100

MINNEHAHA

Launched in 1905, the streetcar boat Minnehaha is now a floating
exhibit and excursion vessel. *City:* Excelsior *State:* MN *Zip:* 55331
Phone: 952-474-2115 *Web:* www.steamboatminnehaha.org *Email:*
mail@steamboatminnehaha.org *Visitors welcome?* Yes *Hours:* Contact
attraction directly *Admission:* Contact attraction directly *Operated by:*
Museum of Lake Minnetonka *NR?* No *NHL?* No *Built:* 1905
Latitude: 44.9033 *Longitude:* -93.5663

PLOVER

Launched in 1944, the foot ferry Plover is now an operating museum
vessel. *Address:* 235 Marine Dr. *City:* Blaine *State:* WA *Zip:* 98230
Phone: 360-332-5742 *Visitors welcome?* Yes *Hours:* Memorial Day
through Labor Day: Call for sailings *Admission:* Children under 12,
FREE; Youth, $1; Adults $5 *Operated by:* Drayton Harbor Maritime
NR? *Yes* *NHL?* No *Built:* 1944 *Latitude:* 48.9945 *Longitude:* -122.7590

SKANSONIA

Launched in 1949, the car ferry Skansonia is a now a floating
restaurant and site for weddings. *Address:* 205 NE Northlake Way

City: Seattle *State:* WA *Zip:* 98105 *Phone:* 206-545-9109 *Web:* https://landmarkeventco.com/skansonia *Email:* info@landmarkeventco.com *Visitors welcome?* Yes *Hours:* Contact attraction directly *Admission:* Contact attraction directly *Operated by:* Landmark Event Company *NR?* No *NHL?* No *Built:* 1949 *Latitude:* 47.6532 *Longitude:* -122.3260

YANKEE

Launched in 1907, the passenger ferry Yankee is now a museum vessel. *Address:* Canal Street Station *City:* New York *State:* NY *Zip:* 10003 *Phone:* 646-265-8788 *Web:* www.mackenziechildsyankeeferry.com *Email:* victoria@yankeeferry.nyc *Visitors welcome?* Yes *Hours:* Contact attraction directly *Admission:* Contact attraction directly *Operated by:* Victoria MacKenzie-Childs **NR? Yes** *NHL?* No *Built:* 1907 *Latitude:* 40.7219 *Longitude:* -74.0054

Fireboats

DUWAMISH

Launched in 1909, the fireboat Duwamish is now a floating museum exhibit and education vessel. *Address:* 860 Terry Ave. N. *City:* Seattle *State:* WA *Zip:* 93777 *Phone:* 206-999-5107 *Web:* fireboatduwamish.com *Email:* mvduwamish@gmail.com *Visitors welcome?* Yes *Hours:* Contact attraction directly *Admission:* Donation *Operated by:* Puget Sound Fireboat Foundation *NR?* No **NHL? Yes** *Built:* 1909 *Latitude:* 47.6276 *Longitude:* -122.3370

EDWARD M. COTTER

Launched in 1900, the fireboat Edward M. Cotter is a working vessel on Buffalo's waterfront. *Address:* 155 Ohio St. *City:* Buffalo *State:* NY *Zip:* 14203 *Phone:* 716-846-4265 *Web:* www.emcotter.com *Visitors welcome?* Yes *Hours:* Contact attraction directly *Admission:* Contact attraction directly *Operated by:* Friends of the Edward M. Cotter *NR?* No **NHL? Yes** *Built:* 1900 *Latitude:* 42.8721 *Longitude:* -78.8721

FIREBOAT NO. 1

Launched in 1929, Fireboat No. 1 is now a dry-berth exhibit at a waterfront park in Tacoma. *Address:* 3300 Ruston Way *City:* Tacoma *State:* WA *Visitors welcome?* Yes *Hours:* Daily *Admission:* FREE *Operated by:* Metro Parks Tacoma *NR?* No **NHL? Yes** *Built:* 1929 *Latitude:* 47.2817 *Longitude:* -122.4800

FIRE FIGHTER

Launched in 1938, Fire Fighter is the most decorated fireboat in the United States. She is now a museum ship. *Address:* Mitchell Park Marina *City:* Greenport *State:* NY *Zip:* 11944 *Web:* americasfireboat.org *Visitors welcome?* Yes *Hours:* Saturdays and Sundays, noon to 5 p.m. *Admission:* Contact attraction directly *NR?* No **NHL? Yes** *Built:* 1938 *Latitude:* 41.1017 *Longitude:* -72.3633

FRED A. BUSSE

Named for a former Chicago mayor, the Fred A Busse was converted from a city fireboat to an excursion vessel. *Address:* 111 N. Lakeshore Dr. *City:* Chicago *State:* IL *Zip:* 60601 Phone 312-919-3367 *Web:* fireboattours.com *Email:* info@fireboattours.com *Visitors welcome?* Yes *Hours:* Contact attraction directly *Admission:* Contact attraction directly *NR?* No *NHL?* No *Built:* 1936 *Latitude:* 41.8839 *Longitude:* -87.6141

JOHN J. HARVEY

Launched in 1931, the fireboat John J. Harvey is now a floating museum in New York Harbor. *Address:* Pier 66 *City:* New York *State:* NY *Web:* www.fireboat.org *Visitors welcome?* Yes *Hours:* Contact attraction directly *Admission:* Contact attraction directly *Operated by:* Save Our Ships New York *NR?* No *NHL?* No *Built:* 1931 *Latitude:* 40.9233 *Longitude:* -73.9047

MAYOR THOMAS D'ALESANDRO, JR.

The fireboat Mayor Thomas D'Alexandro, Jr. is a dry-berth exhibit undergoing restoration in Lutherville, Md. *Address:* 1301 York Road *City:* Lutherville *State:* MD *Zip:* 21093 *Phone:* 410-321-7500 *Web:* www.firemuseummd.org *Email:* sgheaver@firemuseummd.org *Visitors welcome?* Yes *Hours:* Wednesday to Saturday, 10 a.m. to 4 p.m. *Admission:* $15 adults, $13 seniors/firefighters, $7 children age two 18, under two FREE *Operated by:* The Fire Museum of Maryland *Built:*

1956 *NR?* No *NHL?* No *Latitude:* 39.4179 *Longitude:* -76.6167

RALPH J. SCOTT

Launched in 1925, the fireboat Ralph J. Scott is dry-berthed on the Los Angeles waterfront. *Address:* LAFD, Fire Station 112, 444 South Harbor Blvd, Berth 86 *City:* San Pedro *State:* CA *Phone:* 213-978-3800 *Web:* www.lafd.org *Visitors welcome?* Yes *Hours:* Contact attraction directly *Admission:* Contact attraction directly *Operated by:* City of Los Angeles Fire Department **NR? Yes NHL? Yes** *Built:* 1925 *Latitude:* 33.7359 *Longitude:* -118.2920

Fishing Boats

ALOHA

Launched in 1937, the fishing boat Aloha is now a dry-berth exhibit at the Sleeping Bear Dunes National Lakeshore visitor's center. *Address:* 9922 Front St. *City:* Empire *State:* MI *Zip:* 49630 *Phone:* 616-326-5134 *Web:* www.nps.gov/SLBE/ *Visitors welcome?* Yes *Hours:* Daily *Admission:* FREE *Operated by:* Sleeping Bear Dunes National Lakeshore *NR?* No *NHL?* No *Built:* 1937 *Latitude:* 44.8111 *Longitude:* -86.0506

BUDDY O

Launched in 1936, the fish tug Buddy O. is a dry-berth exhibit at the Rogers Street Fishing Village Museum. *Address:* 2010 Rogers St. *City:* Two Rivers *State:* WI *Zip:* 54241 *Phone:* 920-793-5905 *Web:* www.rogersstreet.com *Email:* info@rogersstreet.com *Visitors welcome?* Yes *Hours:* May to October: Daily, 10 a.m. to 4 p.m. *Admission:* Contact attraction directly *Operated by:* Rogers Street Fishing Village & Great Lakes Coast Guard Museum *NR?* No *NHL?* No *Built:* 1936 *Latitude:* 44.1518 *Longitude:* -87.5626

HOPE

The fish tug Hope was built in 1930 by the Sturgeon Bay Boat Works and operated in Lake Michigan until 1992. *Address:* 12724 E Wisconsin Bay Rd *City:* Gills Rock *State:* WI *Zip:* 54210 *Phone:* 920-854-1844 *Web:* www.dcmm.org *Email:* info@dcmm.org *Visitors welcome?* Yes *Hours:* Daily, 10 a.m. to 5 p.m. *Admission:* $6 adults, $3 youth 5-17, children under four FREE *Operated by:* Door County Maritime Museum & Lighthouse Preservation Society *NR?* No *NHL?* No *Built:* 1930 *Latitude:* 45.2905 *Longitude:* -87.0095

ELEANOR D

Launched in 1948, the fishboat Eleanor D. is undergoing restoration at the H. Lee White Marine Museum. *Address:* West 1st Street Pier *City:* Oswego *State:* NY *Zip:* 13126 *Phone:* 315-342-0480 *Web:* www.hleewhitemarinemuseum.com *Email:* info@hleewhitemarinemuseum.com *Visitors welcome?* Yes *Hours:* Daily, 10 a.m. to 5 p.m. *Admission:* $8 adults, $4 youth, children 12 and under FREE *Operated by:* H. Lee White Marine Museum *NR?* No *NHL?* No *Built:* 1948 *Latitude:* 43.4553 *Longitude:* -76.5105

EVELYN S

Launched in 1939, the fish tug Evelyn S. is a dry-berth exhibit at the Michigan Maritime Museum. *Address:* 260 Dyckman Ave. *City:* South Haven *State:* MI *Zip:* 49090 *Phone:* 269-637-8078 *Web:* michiganmaritimemuseum.org *Visitors welcome?* Yes *Hours:* Memorial Day to Labor Day: Daily, 10 a.m. to 5 p.m. *Admission:* $8 adults; $7 seniors, veterans, active military; $5 children; under four FREE *Operated by:* Michigan Maritime Museum *NR?* No *NHL?* No *Built:* 1939 *Latitude:* 42.4070 *Longitude:* -86.2745

FLORENCE

Built in 1926, Florence represents a transition from sail-powered fishing vessels to engine power. She's now in the collection of Mystic Seaport. *Address:* 75 Greenmanville Avenue *City:* Mystic *State:* CT *Zip:* 06355 *Phone:* 860-572-5315 *Web:* www.mysticseaport.org *Visitors welcome?* Yes *Hours:* Thursday to Sunday, 10 a.m. to 4 p.m. *Admission:* $23.95 adults; $21.95 seniors; $19.95 youth 13-17; $16.95 child 4-12 *Operated by:* Mystic Seaport: The Museum of America and the Sea **NR? Yes NHL? Yes** *Built:* 1926 *Latitude:* 41.3617 *Longitude:* -71.9634

FOGGY RIVER

Launched in 1962, the chunk-stern deadrise Foggy River is undergoing restoration at the Reedville Fisherman's Museum. *Address:* 504 Main Street *City:* Reedville *State:* VA *Zip:* 22539 *Phone:*

804-453-6529 *Web:* www.rfmuseum.org *Visitors welcome?* Yes *Hours:* Thursday to Saturday, 11 a.m. to 4 p.m. *Admission:* $5 adults, $3 seniors, children 12 and under FREE *Operated by:* Reedville Fisherman's Museum *NR?* No *NHL?* No *Built:* 1962 *Latitude:* 37.8454 *Longitude:* -76.2742

JACOB PIKE

The 83-foot Jacob Pike is a 1949 sardine carrier that was based in Rockland, Maine. *Address:* 40 E. Main Street *City:* Searsport *State:* ME *Zip:* 04974 *Phone:* 207-548-2297 *Web:* www.penobscotmarinemuseum.org *Email:* admissions@pmm-maine.org *Visitors welcome?* Yes *Hours:* Contact attraction directly *Admission:* Contact attraction directly *Operated by:* Penobscot Marine Museum *NR?* No *NHL?* No *Built:* 1949 *Latitude:* 44.4209 *Longitude:* -69.0006

JOHN N. COBB

Launched in 1950, the John N. Cobb is a former research vessel that is now used as a fishing vessel. *City:* Winchester Bay *State:* OR *Visitors welcome?* No *Hours:* Contact attraction directly *Admission:* Contact attraction directly *Operated by:* Ron Sloan Mar **NR? Yes** *NHL?* No *Built:* 1950 *Latitude:* 43.6771 *Longitude:* -124.1748

HALF SHELL

Launched in 1928, the buyboat Half Shell is now an environmental education training vessel operated by the Matthew Henson Earth Conservation Center of the Earth Conservation Corps. *Address:* 2000 Half Street SW *City:* Washington *State:* DC *Zip:* 20024 *Phone:* 202-479-4505 *Web:* earthconservationcorps.info *Email:* admin@earthconservationcorps.org *Visitors welcome?* Yes *Hours:* Contact attraction directly *Admission:* Contact attraction directly *Operated by:* Earth Conservation Corps *NR?* No *NHL?* No *Built:* 1928 *Latitude:* 38.8661 *Longitude:* -77.0107

KATHERINE V

The Katherine V is believed to be the last wooden fish tug on the Great Lakes. *Address:* 491 Johnson St. *City:* Alpena *State:* MI *Zip:* 49707 *Phone:* 989-356-2202 *Web:* bessermuseum.org *Visitors welcome?*

Yes *Hours:* Monday to Saturday, 10 a.m. to 4 p.m., Sunday, noon to 4 p.m. *Admission:* $5 adults, $3 seniors, children six to 18 children under five FREE *Operated by* Besser Museum **NR?** **Yes** *NHL?* No *Built:* 1928 *Latitude:* 45.0806 *Longitude:* -83.4507

NORDIC SPIRIT

The Nordic Spirit is a Norwegian fishing boat constructed around the turn of the 20th century. Donated to the National Nordic Museum in the 1980s, it sat unused until 2008, when museum supporters set out to refurbish it for the 100th anniversary of the 1909 Alaska-Yukon-Pacific Exposition. *Address:* 2655 NW Market Street *City:* Seattle *State:* WA *Zip:* 98107 *Phone:* 206-789-5707 *Web:* www.nordicmuseum.org *Visitors welcome?* Yes *Hours:* Tuesday to Sunday, 10 a.m. to 5 p.m. *Admission:* $18 adults, $15 students, seniors, $10 children 5 to 18, under five FREE *Operated by:* National Nordic Museum *NR?* No *NHL?* No *Latitude:* 47.6777 *Longitude:* -122.3970

OLD POINT

Old Point is an example of a crabbing dredge boat that harvested Chesapeake Bay crabs in the winter, fish in the summer, and oysters in the fall. *Address:* 213 N. Talbot Street *City:* St. Michaels *State:* MD *Zip:* 21663 *Phone:* 410-745-2916 *Web:* www.cbmm.org *Email:* cbland@cbmm.org *Visitors welcome?* Yes *Hours:* Daily, hours vary by season *Admission:* $16 adults; $13 seniors over 62, students; $12 retired military; $6 kids 6 to 17; active military, kids under 6 FREE *Operated by:* Chesapeake Bay Maritime Museum *NR?* No *NHL?* No *Latitude:* 38.7876 *Longitude:* -76.2249

PENGUIN

Launched in 1935, the deadrise workboat Penguin is a dry-berth exhibit at the Calvert Marine Museum. *Address:* 14200 Solomons Island Road *City:* Solomons *State:* MD *Zip:* 20688 *Phone:* 410-326-2042 *Web:* www.calvertmarinemuseum.com *Email:* Kathleen.Porecki@calvertcountymd.gov *Visitors welcome?* Yes *Hours:* Daily, 10 a.m to 5 p.m. *Admission:* $9 adults, $7 seniors, $4 children 5 to 12; under five FREE *Operated by:* Calvert Marine Museum *NR?* No *NHL?* No *Built:* 1935 *Latitude:* 38.3332 *Longitude:* -76.4720

ROANN

Roann is one of the few surviving examples of eastern-rig draggers that replaced sailing schooners. She was launched in 1944. *Address:* 75 Greenmanville Avenue *City:* Mystic *State:* CT *Zip:* 06355 *Phone:* 860-572-5315 *Web:* www.mysticseaport.org *Visitors welcome?* Yes *Hours:* Thursday to Sunday, 10 a.m. to 4 p.m. *Admission:* $23.95 adults; $21.95 seniors; $19.95 youth 13-17; $16.95 child 4-12 *Operated by:* Mystic Seaport: The Museum of America and the Sea **NR? Yes NHL? Yes** *Built:* 1944 *Latitude:* 41.3617 *Longitude:* -71.9634

SANTA MARIA

Launched in 1937, the restored shrimp boat Santa Maria is part of the Texas Seaport Museum collection. *Address:* Pier 21, Number 8 *City:* Galveston *State:* TX *Zip:* 77550 *Phone:* 409-763-1877 *Web:* www.tsm-elissa.org *Email:* elissa@galvestonhistory.org *Visitors welcome?* Yes *Hours:* Daily, 10 a.m. to 5 p.m. *Admission:* $6 adults, $4.50 students six through 18, children five and under FREE *Operated by:* Galveston Historical Foundation *NR?* No *NHL?* No *Built:* 1937 *Latitude:* 29.3263 *Longitude:* -94.7951

SCRANTON

The shrimp boat Scranton is now a floating museum in the city of Pascagoula. *Address:* Pascagoula River Park *City:* Pascagoula *State:* MS *Zip:* 39567 *Phone:* 228-938-6612 *Visitors welcome?* Yes *Hours:* Fridays and Saturdays, 10 a.m. to 5 p.m. *Admission:* $2 adults, $1 children *Operated by:* City of Pascagoula *NR?* No *NHL?* No *Latitude:* 30.3743 *Longitude:* -88.5647

SHARK

Launched in 1940, the fish tug Shark is now a dry-berth exhibit at the Gitche Gumee Agate and History Museum. *Address:* E21739 Brazel Street *City:* Grand Marais *State:* MI *Zip:* 49839 *Phone:* 906-494-2590 *Web:* www.agatelady.com *Email:* karen@agatelady.com *Visitors welcome?* Yes *Hours:* Contact attraction directly *Admission:* Contact attraction directly *Operated by:* Gitchee Gumee Agate and History Museum *NR?* No *NHL?* No *Built:* 1940 *Latitude:* 46.6473 *Longitude:* -85.9501

SOUTH TWIN

Launched in 1938, the fish tug South Twin is now a dry-berth exhibit. *City:* Red Cliff *State:* MN *Visitors welcome?* Yes *Hours:* Daily *Admission:* FREE *Operated by:* Cecil Peterson's Grocery *NR?* No *NHL?* No *Built:* 1938 *Latitude:* 47.7782 *Longitude:* -90.1908

SHENANDOAH (FISHING VESSEL)

Launched in 1925, the purse-seiner Shenandoah is the last vessel of her type built at the Skansie Ship Building Company at Gig Harbor, Wash. It is now a dry-berth exhibit. *Address:* 4218 Harborview Dr. *City:* Gig Harbor *State:* WA *Visitors welcome?* Yes *Hours:* Thursday to Saturday, 11 a.m. to 4 p.m. *Admission:* FREE *Operated by:* Harbor History Museum *NR?* No *NHL?* No *Built:* 1925 *Latitude:* 47.3374 *Longitude:* -122.5970

STEPHANIE

Launched in 1917, the fishing vessel Stephanie is undergoing restoration in Eureka, California. *Address:* Eureka Public Marina *City:* Eureka *State:* CA *Zip:* 95501 *Phone:* 707-444-9440 *Web:* www.humboldtbaymaritimemuseum.com *Visitors welcome?* Yes *Hours:* Contact attraction directly *Operated by:* Humboldt Bay Maritime Museum *NR?* No *NHL?* No *Built:* 1917 *Latitude:* 40.7933 *Longitude:* -124.1640

TORDENSKJOLD

Launched in 1911, the halibut schooner Tordenskjold is a floating museum and exhibit in Seattle. *Address:* 860 Terry Ave. N. *City:* Seattle *State:* WA *Zip:* 98109 *Phone:* 206-447-9800 *Web:* www.nwseaport.org *Email:* info@nwseaport.org *Visitors welcome?* Yes *Hours:* Contact attraction directly *Admission:* Donation *Operated by:* Northwest Seaport Maritime Heritage Ctr *NR?* No **NHL? Yes** *Built:* 1911 *Latitude:* 47.6276 *Longitude:* -122.3370

TWILITE

The fish tug Twilite is a dry-berth exhibit at the Little Sand Bay Visitors Center in the Apostle Islands National Lakeshore. *Address:* Little Sand Bay Road *City:* Bayfield *State:* WI *Phone:* 715-779-7007 *Web:* www.nps.gov/apis/ *Visitors welcome?* Yes *Hours:* Contact attraction directly *Admission:* FREE *Operated by:* Apostle Islands National Lakeshore *NR?* No *NHL?* No *Latitude:* 46.9329 *Longitude:* -90.8730

WM. B. TENNISON

Launched in 1899, the buyboat Wm. B. Tennison is now an operational museum vessel. *Address:* 14200 Solomons Island Road *City:* Solomons *State:* MD *Zip:* 20688 *Phone:* 410-326-2042 *Web:* www.calvertmarinemuseum.com *Email:* Kathleen.Porecki@calvertcountymd.gov *Visitors welcome?* Yes *Hours:* Daily, 10 a.m to 5 p.m. *Admission:* $9 adults, $7 seniors, $4 children 5 to 12; under five FREE *Operated by:* Calvert Marine Museum **NR?** **Yes NHL?** **Yes** *Built:* 1899 *Latitude:* 38.3332 *Longitude:* -76.4720

Passenger Steamers and Luxury Liners

AURORA

The Aurora is a mid-20th century luxury liner now undergoing restoration in Stockton, Calif. *Address:* West end of 8 Mile Road *City:* Stockton *State:* CA *Zip:* 95203 *Visitors welcome?* No Contact attraction directly *Admission:* Contact attraction directly *Operated by:* M/V Aurora *NR?* No *NHL?* No *Latitude:* 38.0584 *Longitude:* -121.4989

CATALYST

Launched in 1932, the fantail motor yacht Catalyst operates as an excursion vessel in Washington, British Columbia, and Alaska. *City:* Friday Harbor *State:* WA *Zip:* 98250 *Phone:* 360-378-7123 *Web:* www.pacificcatalyst.com *Email:* info@pacificcatalyst.com *Visitors welcome?* Yes *Hours:* Contact attraction directly *Operated by:* Pacific Catalyst II, Inc. *NR?* No *NHL?* No *Built:* 1932 *Latitude:* 48.5343 *Longitude:* -123.0170

COLUMBIA

Launched in 1920, the passenger steamer Columbia is undergoing restoration in Buffalo, New York. *Address:* 8 East 8th Street, #1C *City:* New York *State:* NY *Phone:* 203-499-8204 *Web:* www.sscolumbia.org *Visitors welcome?* No *Hours:* Contact attraction directly *Operated by:* S.S. Columbia Project *NR?* No *NHL?* No *Built:*

1902 *Latitude:* 42.8864 *Longitude:* -78.8784

HELENE

Launched in 1927, the yacht Helene is now derelict. *Address:* 14441 Harbor Island *City:* Detroit *State:* MI *Zip:* 48215 *Phone:* 313-822-0225 *Visitors welcome?* Yes *Hours:* Contact attraction directly *Operated by:* Shamrock Chartering *NR?* No *NHL?* No *Built:* 1927 *Latitude:* 42.3598 *Longitude:* -82.9358

IDA MAY

Launched in 1926, the yacht Ida May is now an excursion vessel. *City:* San Rafael *State:* CA *Phone:* 415-459-6933 *Visitors welcome?* Yes *Hours:* Contact attraction directly *Operated by:* Historic Charters *NR?* No *NHL?* No *Built:* 1926 *Latitude:* 37.9735 *Longitude:* -122.5310

KATAHDIN

Launched in 1914, the steam passenger vessel Katahdin now operates as an excursion vessel on Moosehead Lake. *Address:* 12 Lily Bay Road *City:* Greenville *State:* ME *Zip:* 04441 *Phone:* 207-695-2716 *Web:* www.katahdincruises.com *Email:* info@katahdincruises.com *Visitors welcome?* Yes *Hours:* Contact attraction directly *Operated by:* Moosehead Marine Museum **NR? Yes** *NHL?* No *Built:* 1914 *Latitude:* 45.4595 *Longitude:* -69.5906

MEDEA

Launched in 1904, the steam yacht Medea is now used as an excursion vessel by the Maritime Museum of San Diego. *Address:* 1492 North Harbor Drive *City:* San Diego *State:* CA *Zip:* 92101 *Phone:* 619-234-9153 *Web:* www.sdmaritime.com *Email:* info@sdmaritime.org *Visitors welcome?* Yes *Hours:* Daily, 10 a.m. to 8 p.m. *Admission:* $20 18+; $15 seniors, military, students; $10 children three to 12; children under two FREE *Operated by:* Maritime Museum Association of San Diego *NR?* No *NHL?* No *Built:* 1904 *Latitude:* 32.7276 *Longitude:* -117.1800

MILWAUKEE CLIPPER

Launched in 1905, the passenger steamer Milwaukee Clipper is now a floating museum. *Address:* 2098 Lakeshore Dr. *City:* Muskegon *State:*

MI *Zip:* 49441 *Phone:* 231-722-3533 *Web:* www.milwaukeeclipper.com *Visitors welcome?* Yes *Hours:* Contact attraction directly *Admission:* Contact attraction directly *Operated by:* S.S. Milwaukee Clipper Preservation *NR?* No *NHL?* No *Built:* 1905 *Latitude:* 43.2345 *Longitude:* -86.2484

MISS ANN

Launched in 1926, the motor yacht Miss Ann is a pleasure cruiser operated by a luxury resort. *Address:* 480 King Carter Dr. *City:* Irvington *State:* VA *Zip:* 22480 *Phone:* 804-438-5000 *Web:* www.tidesinn.com *Email:* concierge@tidesinn.com *Visitors welcome?* Yes *Hours:* Contact attraction directly *Operated by:* Tides Inn **NR? Yes** *NHL?* No *Built:* 1926 *Latitude:* 37.6629 *Longitude:* -76.4283

OSPREY

Built in 1881, the steam launch Osprey is a dry-berth exhibit at the Adirondack Experience museum. *Address:* Route 28N/30 *City:* Blue Mountain Lake *State:* NY *Zip:* 12812 *Phone:* 518-352-7311 *Web:* www.theadkx.org *Email:* info@theadkx.org *Visitors welcome?* Yes *Hours:* Contact attraction directly *Admission:* Contact attraction directly *Operated by:* Adirondack Experience *NR?* No *NHL?* No *Built:* 1881 *Latitude:* 43.8728 *Longitude:* -74.4509

POTOMAC

Launched in 1934, the presidential yacht USS Potomac is now an excursion and museum vessel also used for educational programs. *Address:* Jack London Square *City:* Oakland *State:* CA *Zip:* 94607 *Phone:* 510-627-1215 *Web:* www.usspotomac.org *Email:* info@usspotomac.org *Visitors welcome?* Yes *Hours:* Contact attraction directly *Operated by:* USS Potomac Association **NR? Yes NHL? Yes** *Built:* 1934 *Latitude:* 37.7942 *Longitude:* -122.2760

QUEEN MARY

Launched in 1936, the luxury passenger liner Queen Mary is now a floating exhibit in Long Beach, Calif. *Address:* 1126 Queen's Highway *City:* Long Beach *State:* CA *Zip:* 90802 *Phone:* 562-435-3510 *Web:* www.queenmary.com *Visitors welcome?* Yes *Hours:* Contact attraction directly *Admission:* Contact attraction directly *Operated by:* Queen Mary

NR? **Yes** *NHL?* No *Built:* 1936 *Latitude:* 33.7526 *Longitude:* -118.1900

SABINO

Launched in 1908, the passenger vessel Sabino is an operational part of the Mystic Seaport museum program. *Address:* 75 Greenmanville Avenue *City:* Mystic *State:* CT *Zip:* 06355 *Phone:* 860-572-5315 *Web:* www.mysticseaport.org *Visitors welcome?* Yes *Hours:* Thursday to Sunday, 10 a.m. to 4 p.m. *Admission:* $23.95 adults; $21.95 seniors; $19.95 youth 13-17; $16.95 child 4-12 *Operated by:* Mystic Seaport: The Museum of America and the Sea *NR?* **Yes** *NHL?* **Yes** *Built:* 1908 *Latitude:* 41.3617 *Longitude:* -71.9634

> Several historic passenger vessels still run regular routes in their communities. Call or visit their websites for the sailing schedule.

STE. CLAIRE

Launched in 1910, the passenger steamer Ste. Claire is undergoing restoration near Detroit. *Address:* 11000 Freud St *City:* Detroit *State:* MI *Zip:* 48214 *Web:* bobloboat.com *Email:* mrlee@bobloboat.com *Visitors welcome?* Yes *Hours:* Contact attraction directly *Admission:* Contact attraction directly *Operated by:* Bob-Lo Boat *NR?* No *NHL?* **Yes** *Built:* 1910 *Latitude:* 42.3570 *Longitude:* -82.9678

TICONDEROGA

Launched in 1906, the passenger steamer Ticonderoga is a dry-berth exhibit at the Shelburne Museum. *Address:* 5555 Shelburne Rd. *City:* Shelburne *State:* VT *Zip:* 05482 *Phone:* 802-985-3346 *Web:* www.shelburnemuseum.org *Email:* info@shelburnemuseum.org *Visitors welcome?* Yes *Hours:* Wednesday to Sunday, 10 a.m. to 4 p.m. *Admission:* Contact attraction directly *Operated by:* Shelburne Museum *NR?* **Yes** *NHL?* **Yes** *Built:* 1906 *Latitude:* 44.3768 *Longitude:* -73.2285

UNITED STATES

Launched in 1952, the SS United States was the last and greatest of the large American-built ocean liners built in the years before commercial airplanes became the main mode of transatlantic and transpacific travel. *Address:* Pier 82 *City:* Philadelphia *State:* PA *Web:* www.ssunitedstatesconservancy.org *Email:* info@ssusc.org *Visitors welcome?* No *Operated by:* SS United States Conservancy *NR?* No *NHL?* No *Built:* 1952 *Latitude:* 39.9180 *Longitude:* -75.1369

VIRGINIA V

Launched in 1922, the passenger steamer Virginia V is now a museum ship and excursion vessel. *Address:* 860 Terry Ave. N. *City:* Seattle *State:* WA *Zip:* 98109 *Phone:* 206-624-9119 *Web:* www.virginiav.org *Email:* info@virginiav.org *Visitors welcome?* Yes *Hours:* Contact attraction directly *Operated by:* Steamer Virginia V Foundation **NR? Yes NHL? Yes** *Built:* 1922 *Latitude:* 47.6276 *Longitude:* -122.3370

Speciality Vessels

BAY ARK

Launched approximately 1896, the houseboat Bay Ark, also called the Lewis Ark, is now a dry-berthed museum vessel at the San Francisco Maritime National Historical Park. *Address:* San Francisco Maritime National Historical Park *City:* San Francisco *State:* CA *Zip:* 94123 *Phone:* 415-561-7006 *Web:* www.nps.gov/safr/ *Visitors welcome?* Yes *Hours:* Contact attraction directly *Admission:* $15 *Operated by:* San Francisco Maritime National Historical Park *NR?* No *NHL?* No *Built:* 1896 *Latitude:* 37.8070 *Longitude:* -122.4220

CANTON

The 32-foot U.S. Army Corps of Engineers workboat Canton is part of the collection of the Mississippi River Museum. *Address:* 350 East Third St. *City:* Dubuque *State:* IA *Zip:* 52001 *Phone:* 563-557-9545 *Web:* www.rivermuseum.com *Visitors welcome?* Yes *Hours:* Daily, 9 a.m. to 5 p.m. *Admission:* $19.95 adults, $17.95 seniors, $14.95 youth three to 17 *Operated by:* Dubuque County Historical Society *NR?* No *NHL?* No *Latitude:* 42.4963 *Longitude:* -90.6591

CAPTAIN MERIWETHER LEWIS

Launched in 1932, the self-propelled dustpan dredge Captain Meriweather Lewis is now a dry-berth exhibit and a museum. *Address:* Nebraska Ave & E Allen St. *City:* Brownville *State:* NE *Zip:* 68321 *Phone:* 402-825-6001 *Web:* lewisdredge.org *Email:*

LewisDredgeFoundation@gmail.com *Visitors welcome?* Yes *Hours:* Contact attraction directly *Admission:* Contact attraction directly *Operated by:* Captain Meriwether Lewis Foundation **NR? Yes NHL? Yes** *Built:* 1932 *Latitude:* 40.3933 *Longitude:* -95.6548

CHUGACH

Launched in 1925, the ranger boat Chugach is a working vessel owned by the U.S. Forest Service. *Address:* Front St. *City:* Wrangell *State:* AK *Zip:* 99929 *Phone:* 907-874-3736 *Visitors welcome?* Yes *Hours:* Contact attraction directly *Admission:* Contact attraction directly *Operated by:* Tongass National Forest **NR? Yes** NHL? No *Built:* 1925 *Latitude:* 56.4708 *Longitude:* -132.3767

DERRICK BARGE NO. 8

Launched in 1925, Derrick Barge No. 8 is in the collection of the H. Lee White Marine Museum. *Address:* West 1st Street Pier *City:* Oswego *State:* NY *Zip:* 13126 *Phone:* 315-342-0480 *Web:* www.hleewhitemarinemuseum.com *Email:* info@hleewhitemarinemuseum.com *Visitors welcome?* Yes *Hours:* Daily, 10 a.m. to 5 p.m. *Admission:* $8 adults, $4 youth, children 12 and under FREE *Operated by:* H. Lee White Marine Museum *NR?* No *NHL?* No *Built:* 1925 *Latitude:* 43.4553 *Longitude:* -76.5105

GOLDSTREAM DREDGE NO. 8

Launched in 1928, the Goldstream Dredge No. 8 is a gold mining dredge that is at the center of a National Historic District. *Address:* 1755 Old Steese Hwy N. *City:* Fairbanks *State:* AK *Zip:* 99712 *Phone:* 907-479-6673 *Web:* www.golddredge8.com *Email:* info@golddredge8.com *Visitors welcome?* Yes *Hours:* Daily *Admission:* Contact attraction directly *Operated by:* Gold Dredge No. 8 **NR? Yes** NHL? No *Built:* 1928 *Latitude:* 64.9417 *Longitude:* -147.6560

GYRFALCON

Launched in 1981, the Viking faering boat Gyrfalcon is a replica of a traditional Viking four-oared vessel. It is used as a living history exhibit. *City:* Oakley *State:* MD *Phone:* 301-390-4089 *Web:* www.longshipco.org *Email:* longshipco@hotmail.com *Visitors welcome?* Yes *Hours:* Contact attraction directly *Admission:* Contact attraction directly *Operated by:* Longship Company *NR?* No *NHL?* No *Built:* 1981 *Latitude:* 38.2729 *Longitude:* -76.7397

HJEMKOMST

Launched in 1980, the replica Viking ship Hjemkomst was built and sailed by a local high school teacher. The ship is now part of the Hjemkomst Center. *Address:* 202 First Avenue N. *City:* Moorhead *State:* MN *Zip:* 56560 *Phone:* 218-299-5515 *Web:* www.hjemkomst-center.com *Visitors welcome?* Yes *Hours:* Monday to Sunday, noon to 5 p.m. *Admission:* Contact attraction directly *Operated by:* Historical and Cultural Society of Clay County *NR?* No *NHL?* No *Built:* 1980 *Latitude:* 46.8771 *Longitude:* -96.7773

LA DUCHESSE

Launched in 1903, the houseboat La Duchesse is a floating exhibit and excursion vessel in Clayton, New York. *Address:* 750 Mary St. *City:* Clayton *State:* NY *Zip:* 13624 *Phone:* 315-686-4104 *Web:* www.abm.org *Email:* rebecca@abm.org *Visitors welcome?* Yes *Hours:* Daily, 9 a.m. to 5 p.m. *Admission:* Contact attraction directly *Operated by:* Antique Boat Museum *NR?* No *NHL?* No *Built:* 1903 *Latitude:* 44.2383 *Longitude:* -76.0893

LEHIGH VALLEY RAILROAD BARGE NO. 79

Launched in 1914, the Lehigh Valley Railroad Barge No. 79 is a floating exhibit for the Waterfront Museum and Showboat Barge. *Address:* 290 Conover St. at Pier 44 *City:* Brooklyn *State:* NY *Zip:* 11231 *Phone:* 718-624-4719 *Web:* www.waterfrontmuseum.org *Email:* dsharps@waterfrontmuseum.org *Visitors welcome?* Yes *Hours:* Thursdays, 4 p.m. to 8 p.m.; Saturdays, 1 p.m. to 5 p.m. *Admission:* By donation *Operated by:* Hudson Waterfront Museum ***NR? Yes*** *NHL?* No *Built:* 1914 *Latitude:* 40.6754 *Longitude:* -74.0174

LOTUS (HOUSEBOAT CRUISER)

Launched in 1909, the houseboat cruiser Lotus is now an excursion vessel. *Address:* Lake Union Park *City:* Seattle *State:* WA *Phone:* 425-243-9641 *Web:* www.mvlotus.org *Email:* info@mvlotus.org *Visitors welcome?* Yes *Hours:* Contact attraction directly *Admission:* Contact attraction directly *Operated by:* MV Lotus Heritage Foundation ***NR?***

Yes NHL? No *Built:* 1909 *Latitude:* 48.1126 *Longitude:* -122.7610

MONTGOMERY

Launched in 1926, the snagboat Montgomery is now a floating exhibit. *Address:* 1382 Lock and Dam Road *City:* Carrollton *State:* AL *Zip:* 35447 *Phone:* 205-373-8705 *Web:* www.sam.usace.army.mil *Visitors welcome?* Yes *Hours:* Summer: Tuesday to Saturday, 9 a.m. to 5 p.m.; Winter: Monday through Friday, 8 a.m. to 4 p.m. *Admission:* FREE *Operated by:* Tom Bevill Visitor Center (USACE) **NR? Yes NHL? Yes** *Built:* 1926 *Latitude:* 33.2184 *Longitude:* -88.2709

MR. CHARLIE

Launched in 1953, the offshore drilling rig Mr. Charlie is now a museum. *Address:* 111 First St. *City:* Morgan City *State:* LA *Zip:* 70381 *Phone:* 985-384-3744 *Web:* www.rigmuseum.com *Email:* rigmuseum@petronet.net *Visitors welcome?* Yes *Hours:* Monday to Saturday, 10 a.m. to 2 p.m. *Admission:* $5 adults, $4 seniors, $3.50 children under 12, under five FREE *Operated by:* International Petroleum Museum & Exposition *NR?* No *NHL?* No *Built:* 1953 *Latitude:* 29.6919 *Longitude:* -91.2083

NORSEMAN

Launched in 1992, the longship Norseman is a living history education vessel. *City:* Swarthmore *State:* PA *Zip:* 19081 *Phone:* 610-476-9842 *Web:* www.vikingship.org *Email:* info@vikingship.org *Visitors welcome?* Yes *Hours:* Contact attraction directly *Admission:* Contact attraction directly *Operated by:* Leif Ericson Viking Ship *NR?* No *NHL?* No *Built:* 1992 *Latitude:* 39.9021 *Longitude:* -75.3499

OCEAN STAR

Launched in 1969, the offshore drilling rig Ocean Star is now a museum on Galveston Island. *Address:* Harborside Drive at 20th Street *City:* Galveston *State:* TX *Zip:* 77550 *Phone:* 409-766-7287 *Web:* www.oceanstaroec.com *Email:* osmuseum@oceanstaroec.com *Visitors welcome?* Yes *Hours:* Thursday to Monday, 10 a.m. to 5 p.m. *Admission:* Contact attraction directly *Operated by:* Offshore Energy Center *NR?* No *NHL?* No *Built:* 1969 *Latitude:* 29.3090 *Longitude:* -94.7912

PERSEVERANCE

The Perseverance is a replica of a colonial era bateau used for military and commercial purposes. *Address:* 4472 Basin Harbor Rd. *City:* Vergennes *State:* VT *Zip:* 05491 *Phone:* 802-475-2022 *Web:* www.lcmm.org *Email:* info@lcmm.org *Visitors welcome?* Yes *Hours:* Contact attraction directly *Admission:* Contact attraction directly *Operated by:* Lake Champlain Maritime Museum *NR?* No *NHL?* No *Built:* 1986 *Latitude:* 44.1973 *Longitude:* -73.3567

PILOT

Launched in 1914, Pilot served as San Diego Bay's pilot transfer vessel for many years. *Address:* 1492 North Harbor Drive *City:* San Diego *State:* CA *Zip:* 92101 *Phone:* 619-234-9153 *Web:* www.sdmaritime.com *Email:* info@sdmaritime.org *Visitors welcome?* Yes *Hours:* Daily, 10 a.m. to 8 p.m. *Admission:* $20 18+; $15 seniors, military, students; $10 children three to 12; children under two FREE *Operated by:* Maritime Museum Association of San Diego *NR?* No *NHL?* No *Built:* 1914 *Latitude:* 32.7276 *Longitude:* -117.1800

PROPELLER

The SSS Propeller is a Sea Scout ship based in the Seattle area. *Address:* N Northlake Way and 36th St *City:* Seattle *State:* WA *Zip:* 98103 *Phone:* 206-355-2033 *Web:* www.sss-propeller.org *Email:* info@sss-propeller.org *Visitors welcome?* Yes *Hours:* Contact attraction directly *Admission:* Contact attraction directly *Operated by:* Sea Scout Ship Propeller *NR?* No *NHL?* No *Latitude:* 47.6509 *Longitude:* -122.3300

SAE HRAFN

Launched in 2004, the Viking longship Sae Hrafn is a replica of a traditional Viking longship. It is used as a living history exhibit. *City:* Oakley *State:* MD *Phone:* 301-390-4089 *Web:* www.longshipco.org *Email:* longshipco@hotmail.com *Visitors welcome?* Yes *Hours:* Contact attraction directly *Admission:* Contact attraction directly *Operated by:* Longship Company *NR?* No *NHL?* No *Built:* 2004 *Latitude:* 38.2729 *Longitude:* -76.7397

SUMPTER VALLEY

Constructed in 1935, the gold dredge Sumpter Valley is within a state park and is a museum. *Address:* 575 SW Dredge Loop Rd. *City:* Sumpter *State:* OR *Zip:* 97877 *Phone:* 541-894-2472 *Web:* www.historicsumpter.com *Visitors welcome?* Yes *Hours:* Monday to Thursday, 10 a.m. to 4 p.m.; Friday to Sunday, 9 a.m. to 5 p.m. *Admission:* Contact attraction directly *Operated by:* Friends of Sumpter Valley Gold Dredge **NR?** **Yes** NHL? No *Built:* 1935 *Latitude:* 44.7883 *Longitude:* -118.2140

W.T. PRESTON

Launched in 1939, the snagboat W.T. Preston is now a dry-berth exhibit. *Address:* 713 R Ave. *City:* Anacortes *State:* WA *Phone:* 360-293-1915 *Web:* www.anacorteswa.gov/333/Museum *Email:* coa.museum@cityofanacortes.org *Visitors welcome?* Yes *Hours:* Tuesday to Saturday, 10 a.m. to 4 p.m. *Admission:* FREE *Operated by:* Anacortes Maritime Heritage Center **NR?** **Yes NHL?** **Yes** *Built:* 1939 *Latitude:* 48.5158 *Longitude:* -122.6090

WILLIAM M. BLACK

Launched in 1934, the hydraulic pipeline dredge William M. Black was one of the last great steam-powered side-wheelers used for dredging operations on the Mississippi River. *Address:* 350 East Third St. *City:* Dubuque *State:* IA *Zip:* 52001 *Phone:* 563-557-9545 Toll-free: 800-226-3369 *Web:* www.rivermuseum.com *Visitors welcome?* Yes *Hours:* Daily, 9 a.m. to 5 p.m. *Admission:* $19.95 adults, $17.95 seniors, $14.95 youth three to 17 *Operated by:* Dubuque County Historical Society **NR?** **Yes NHL?** **Yes** *Built:* 1934 *Latitude:* 42.4963 *Longitude:* -90.6591

YANKEE FORK

Launched in 1940, the gold dredge Yankee Fork is now a museum near Sunbeam, Idaho. *Address:* Yankee Fork Road *City:* Sunbeam *State:* ID *Phone:* 208-838-2529 *Web:* yankeeforkdredge.com *Visitors welcome?* Yes *Hours:* Memorial Day to Labor Day, Saturdays, 10 a.m. to 4:30 p.m. *Admission:* $5 adults, $1 children six to 12, under six FREE *Operated by:* Yankee Fork Gold Dredge NR? No NHL? No *Built:* 1940 *Latitude:* 44.2876 *Longitude:* -114.7260

Steamboats and Sternwheelers

BELLE OF LOUISVILLE

Launched in 1914, the steamboat Belle of Louisville is now a museum ship and river excursion vessel. *Address:* 401 W. River Road *City:* Louisville *State:* KY *Zip:* 40202 *Phone:* 502-574-2992 *Web:* belleoflouisville.org *Visitors welcome?* Yes *Hours:* Contact attraction directly *Operated by:* Belle of Louisville & Spirit of Jefferson Cruises *NR?* **Yes** *NHL?* **Yes** *Built:* 1914 *Latitude:* 38.2589 *Longitude:* -85.7523

CHAUTAUQUA BELLE

The sternwheeler Chautauqua Belle is a private excursion vessel offering steamboat rides. *Address:* McCrea Point Park, 14 Jones and Gifford Ave *City:* Jamestown *State:* NY *Zip:* 14701 *Phone:* 716-269-2355 *Web:* www.269belle.com *Email:* thechautauquabelle@gmail.com *Visitors welcome?* Yes *Hours:* Contact attraction directly *Operated by:* U.S. Steam Lines, Ltd *NR?* No *NHL?* No *Latitude:* 42.2433 *Longitude:* -79.4966

CITY OF CLINTON

Launched in 1935, the showboat City of Clinton is now dry-berthed and used as a theatre. *Address:* 6th Ave. N. and Riverview Dr. *City:* Clinton *State:* IA *Zip:* 52733 *Phone:* 563-242-6760 *Web:* www.clintonshowboat.org *Email:* boxoffice@clintonshowboat.org *Visitors welcome?* Yes *Hours:* Contact attraction directly *Operated by:* Clinton Area Showboat Theatre *NR?* No *NHL?* No *Built:* 1935 *Latitude:* 41.8493 *Longitude:* -90.1830

COLUMBIA GORGE

The reproduction sternwheeler Columbia Gorge is an excursion vessel. *Address:* 1 NW Portage Rd *City:* Cascade Locks *State:* OR *Zip:* 97014 *Phone:* 503-224-3900 *Web:* www.sternwheeler.com *Email:* reservations@portlandspirit.com *Visitors welcome?* Yes *Hours:* Contact attraction directly *Operated by:* Portland Spirit *NR?* No *NHL?* No *Latitude:* 45.6711 *Longitude:* -121.8890

DELTA KING

Launched in 1926, the river steamboat Delta King is a floating hotel in Old Sacramento. *Address:* 1000 Front Street *City:* Sacramento *State:* CA *Zip:* 95814 *Phone:* 916-444-5464 *Web:* www.deltaking.com *Email:* inquiry@deltaking.com *Visitors welcome?* Yes *Hours:* Contact attraction directly *Operated by:* The Delta King Hotel **NR? Yes** NHL? No *Built:* 1926 *Latitude:* 38.5905 *Longitude:* -121.5060

DELTA QUEEN

Launched in 1926, the river steamboat Delta Queen is operated as an excursion vessel on the Mississippi River. *City:* Kimmswick *State:* MO *Zip:* 63053 *Phone:* 636-464-6464 *Web:* deltaqueen.com *Visitors welcome?* Yes *Hours:* Contact attraction directly *Operated by:* Delta Queen Steamboat Company **NR? Yes NHL? Yes** *Built:* 1926 *Latitude:* 38.3662 *Longitude:* -90.3648

MAJESTIC

Launched in 1923, the showboat Majestic is still in use as an entertainment venue at the New Richmond Designated Outdoor Refreshment Area. *City:* New Richmond *State:* OH *Zip:* 45157 *Visitors welcome?* Yes *Hours:* Contact attraction directly Admission: Contact attraction directly. *Operated by:* City of New Richmond **NR? Yes NHL? Yes** *Built:* 1923 *Latitude:* 38.9487 *Longitude:* -84.2799

MARY M. MILLER

Launched in 1985, the steamboat Mary M. Miller is an excursion vessel named for the first licensed female steamboat captain in America. *Address:* 401 W. River Road *City:* Louisville *State:* KY *Zip:* 40202 *Phone:* 502-574-2992 *Web:* belleoflouisville.org *Visitors welcome?* Yes *Hours:* Contact attraction directly *Operated by:* Belle of Louisville & Spirit of Jefferson Cruises **NR? Yes NHL? Yes** *Built:* 1914 *Latitude:* 38.2589 *Longitude:* -85.7523

NENANA

Launched in 1933, the river steamboat Nenana is now a dry-berth exhibit at Alaskaland Park. *Address:* Alaskaland Park *City:* Fairbanks *State:* AK *Zip:* 99707 *Phone:* 907-456-8848 *Visitors welcome?* Yes *Hours:* Contact attraction directly *Operated by:* Fairbanks Historical Preservation Foundation **NR? Yes NHL? Yes** *Built:* 1933 *Latitude:* 64.8390 *Longitude:* -147.7680

SPIRIT OF JEFFERSON

Launched in 1963 as the Mark Twain, the riverboat Spirit of Jefferson is an excursion vessel. *Address:* 401 W. River Road *City:* Louisville *State:* KY *Zip:* 40202 *Phone:* 502-574-2992 *Web:* belleoflouisville.org *Visitors welcome?* Yes *Hours:* Contact attraction directly *Operated by:* Belle of Louisville & Spirit of Jefferson Cruises *NR?* No *NHL?* No *Built:* 1963 *Latitude:* 38.2589 *Longitude:* -85.7523

SUWANEE

Launched in 1928, the sternwheel passenger steamer Suwanee is now an excursion vessel at The Henry Ford: Greenfield Village. *Address:* 20900 Oakwood Blvd. *City:* Dearborn *State:* MI *Zip:* 48124 *Phone:* 313-982-6001 *Web:* www.thehenryford.org *Visitors welcome?* Yes *Hours:* Monday to Friday, 9 a.m. to 5 p.m. *Admission:* Contact attraction directly *Operated by:* Henry Ford Museum: Greenfield Village *NR?* No *NHL?* No *Built:* 1928 *Latitude:* 42.3001 *Longitude:* -83.2329

Submarines

ALUMINAUT

Launched in 1964, the deep submergence vessel Aluminaut is now on display at the Science Museum of Virginia. *Address:* 2500 West Broad St. *City:* Richmond *State:* VA *Zip:* 23220 *Phone:* 804-864-1400 Toll-free: 800-659-1727 *Web:* www.smv.org *Email:* info@smv.org *Visitors welcome?* Yes *Hours:* Wednesday to Sunday, 9:30 a.m. to 5 p.m. *Admission:* $15.50 adults, $13.50 seniors and youth, $10 children three to five, under three FREE *Operated by:* Science Museum of Virginia *NR?* No *NHL?* No *Built:* 1964 *Latitude:* 37.5616 *Longitude:* -77.4660

DEEP QUEST

The research submersible Deep Quest is a dry-berth display at the Naval Undersea Museum near Keyport, Wash. *Address:* 1103 Hunley Road *City:* Silverdale *State:* WA *Zip:* 98315 *Phone:* 360-396-4148 *Web:* www.history.navy.mil/museums/keyport/index1.htm *Visitors welcome?* Yes *Hours:* Summer (June to September): Daily, 10 a.m. to 4 p.m; Winter (October to May): Wednesday to Monday, 10 a.m. to 4 p.m. *Admission:* FREE *Operated by:* Naval History & Heritage

Command *NR?* No *NHL?* No *Latitude:* 47.6980 *Longitude:* -122.6970

FENIAN RAM

Launched in 1881, the experimental submarine Fenian Ram is on exhibit at the Paterson Museum. *Address:* 2 Market Street *City:* Paterson *State:* NJ *Zip:* 07501 *Phone:* 973-321-1260 *Web:* www.thepatersonmuseum.com *Visitors welcome?* Yes *Hours:* Tuesday to Friday, 10 a.m. to 4 p.m., Saturday and Sunday, 12:30 p.m. to 4:30 p.m. *Admission:* $2 adults, children 18 and under FREE *Operated by:* Paterson Museum *NR?* No *NHL?* No *Built:* 1881 *Latitude:* 40.9137 *Longitude:* -74.1792

HOLLAND BOAT NO. 1

Launched in 1878, the experimental submarine Holland Boat No. 1 is on exhibit at the Paterson Museum. *Address:* 2 Market Street *City:* Paterson *State:* NJ *Zip:* 07501 *Phone:* 973-321-1260 *Web:* www.thepatersonmuseum.com *Visitors welcome?* Yes *Hours:* Tuesday to Friday, 10 a.m. to 4 p.m., Saturday and Sunday, 12:30 p.m. to 4:30 p.m. *Admission:* $2 adults, children 18 and under FREE *Operated by:* Paterson Museum *NR?* No *NHL?* No *Built:* 1878 *Latitude:* 40.9137 *Longitude:* -74.1792

TRIESTE

Launched in 1953, the deep submergence vessel Trieste is now a dry-berth exhibit at the Washington Navy Yard. *Address:* 805 Kidder Breese SE, Washington Navy Yard *City:* Washington *State:* DC *Zip:* 20374 *Phone:* 202-433-6897 *Web:* https://www.history.navy.mil/content/history/museums/nmusn.html *Visitors welcome?* Yes *Hours:* Monday to Friday, 9 a.m. to 4 p.m., Saturdays, 10 a.m. to 4 p.m. *Admission:* Contact attraction directly *Operated by:* National Museum of the United States Navy *NR?* No *NHL?* No *Built:* 1953 *Latitude:* 38.8755 *Longitude:* -76.9935

TRIESTE II

Launched in 1953, the deep submergence vessel Trieste II is now a dry-berth exhibit at the Naval Undersea Museum. *Address:* 1 Garnett Way, Washington Navy Yard *City:* Keyport *State:* WA *Zip:* 98345 *Phone:* 360-396-4148 *Web:* www.navalunderseamuseum.org *Visitors welcome?* Yes *Hours:* Daily, 10 a.m. to 4 p.m. *Admission:* FREE *Operated by:* Naval Undersea Museum *NR?* No *NHL?* No *Built:* 1953 *Latitude:* 38.8755 *Longitude:* -76.9935

PRESSED FOR TIME? FYDDEYE RECOMMENDS	
Mary Whalen	Rare preserved tanker
Meteor	Unusual hull design history
Tordenskjold	Working vessel for 100 years
Deep Quest	Important deep-sea research

7

TALL SHIPS

The Star of India in San Diego Bay. She is the world's oldest active ship.
(Photo: Port of San Diego)

Who isn't thrilled by a tall ship with all its sails set? *The Fyddeye Guide to America's Veteran Warships* features a selected number of vessels that provide excursion and educational opportunities. Some are replicas of vessels going back to the 15th century. Ordinary people can sail for a few hours, days or weeks in many of them.

A.J. MEERWALD
Launched in 1928, the Delaware Bay oyster schooner A.J. Meerwald now serves as an operational museum ship. *Address:* 2800 High Street *City:* Port Norris *State:* NJ *Zip:* 08349 *Phone:* 856-785-2060 *Web:*

www.bayshorecenter.org *Email:* info@bayshorecenter.org *Visitors welcome?* Yes *Hours:* Contact attraction directly *Admission:* Contact attraction directly *Operated by:* Bayshore Center at Bivalve **NR? Yes** *NHL?* No *Built:* 1928 *Latitude:* 39.2332 *Longitude:* -75.0336

ADVENTURE (SCHOONER)

Built in 1926, Adventure is a 121-foot fishing schooner and a National Historical Landmark. *Address:* 4 Harbor Loop *City:* Gloucester *State:* MA *Zip:* 01930 *Phone:* 978-281-8079 *Web:* www.schooner-adventure.org *Email:* info@schooner-adventure.org *Visitors welcome?* Yes *Hours:* Contact attraction directly *Admission:* Contact attraction directly *Operated by:* Schooner Adventure *NR?* No **NHL? Yes** *Built:* 1926 *Latitude:* 42.6118 *Longitude:* -70.6607

ADVENTURE (TRADER)

Adventure is a replica of a 17th century trading vessel. *Address:* 1500 Old Towne Road *City:* Charleston *State:* SC *Zip:* 29407 *Phone:* 803-734-0156 *Web:* southcarolinaparks.com/charles-towne-landing *Email:* charlestowne@scprt.com *Visitors welcome?* Yes *Hours:* 9 a.m. to 5 p.m. *Admission:* $12 adult; $7.50 SC senior; $7 youth 6-15; children under 5 FREE. *Operated by:* Friends of Charles Towne Landing *NR?* No *NHL?* No *Latitude:* 32.8100 *Longitude:* -79.9953

ADVENTURESS

Launched in 1913, the schooner Adventuress is an excursion and environmental education vessel in Puget Sound. *Address:* Water St. and Polk St. *City:* Port Townsend *State:* WA *Zip:* 98368 *Phone:* 360-379-0438 *Web:* www.soundexp.org *Email:* mail@soundexp.org *Visitors welcome?* Yes *Hours:* Contact attraction directly *Admission:* Contact attraction directly *Operated by:* Sound Experience *NR?* No **NHL? Yes** *Built:* 1913 *Latitude:* 48.1136 *Longitude:* -122.7590

ALABAMA (SCHOONER)

Launched in 1926, the schooner Alabama is now an excursion and sail training vessel. *City:* Vineyard Haven *State:* MA *Zip:* 02568 *Phone:* 508-693-1699 *Web:* www.theblackdogtallships.com *Email:* office@theblackdogtallships.com *Visitors welcome?* Yes *Hours:* Contact attraction directly *Admission:* Contact attraction directly *Operated by:*

Black Dog Tall Ship Co. *NR?* No *NHL?* No *Built:* 1926 *Latitude:* 41.4543 *Longitude:* -70.6036

ALICE E

Launched in 1899 and now an excursion vessel, the friendship sloop Alice E. is the oldest working vessel of her type. *Address:* Dysart's Great Harbor Marina, 11 Apple Lane *City:* Southwest Harbor *State:* ME *Zip:* 04679 *Phone:* 207-266-5210 *Web:* www.downeastfriendshipsloop.com *Email:* sailacadia@gmail.com *Visitors welcome?* Yes *Hours:* Contact attraction directly *Admission:* Contact attraction directly *Operated by:* Downeast Friendship Sloop Charters *NR?* No *NHL?* No *Built:* 1899 *Latitude:* 44.2986 *Longitude:* -68.3624

ALLIANCE

Launched in 1995, the schooner Alliance is an excursion and sail training vessel. *Address:* 425 Water St. *City:* Yorktown *State:* VA *Zip:* 23690 *Phone:* 757-639-1233 *Web:* sailyorktown.com *Email:* info@sailyorktown.com *Visitors welcome?* Yes *Hours:* Contact attraction directly *Admission:* Contact attraction directly *Operated by:* Yorktown Sailing Charters *NR?* No *NHL?* No *Built:* 1995 *Latitude:* 37.2700 *Longitude:* -76.0151

Most tall ships, especially schooners, are working vessels that may be out sailing when you want to visit. Always visit the ship's website or call to ensure its availability to you.

ALMA

Launched in 1891, the scow schooner Alma is an operational museum ship at the San Francisco National Maritime Historical Park. *Address:* San Francisco Maritime National Historical Park *City:* San Francisco *State:* CA *Zip:* 94123 *Phone:* 415-561-7006 *Web:* www.nps.gov/safr/ *Visitors welcome?* Yes *Hours:* 8 a.m. to 5 p.m. *Admission:* $15 adults *Operated by:* San Francisco Maritime National Historical Park **NR? Yes NHL? Yes** *Built:* 1891 *Latitude:* 37.8096 *Longitude:* -122.4210

AMAZING GRACE

The schooner Amazing Grace is an excursion vessel and leadership training facility. *City:* Fajardo *State:* PR *Zip:* 00738 *Phone:* 787-860-3434 *Web:* www.eastislandpr.com/charters/amazing-grace *Email:* info@eastislandpr.com *Visitors welcome?* Yes *Hours:* Contact attraction directly *Admission:* Contact attraction directly *Operated by:* East Island Excursions *NR?* No *NHL?* No *Latitude:* 18.2872 *Longitude:* -65.6360

AMERICAN

Launched in 1934, the schooner American is now berthed next to a restaurant in Cape May. *Address:* Fisherman's Wharf, Cape May Harbor *City:* Cape May *State:* NJ *Phone:* 609-884-8296 *Web:* www.thelobsterhouse.com *Visitors welcome?* Yes *Hours:* Contact attraction directly *Admission:* Contact attraction directly *Operated by:* Lobster House *NR?* No *NHL?* No *Built:* 1934 *Latitude:* 38.9351 *Longitude:* -74.9060

AMERICAN EAGLE

Launched in 1930, the auxiliary schooner American Eagle began as a fishing vessel and now operates as an excursion ship. *Address:* 5 Achorn Street *City:* Rockland *State:* ME *Zip:* 04841 *Phone:* 207-594-8007 Toll-free: 800-648-4544 *Web:* www.schooneramericaneagle.com *Email:* info@schooneramericaneagle.com *Visitors welcome?* Yes *Hours:* Contact attraction directly *Admission:* Contact attraction directly *Operated by:* North End Shipyard Schooners **NR? Yes NHL? Yes** *Built:* 1930 *Latitude:* 44.1127 *Longitude:* -69.1049

AMERICAN PRIDE

Launched in 1941, the schooner American Pride is an excursion and sail training vessel. *Address:* Berth 73, Suite 2 *City:* San Pedro *State:* CA *Phone:* 310-833-6055 *Web:* lamitopsail.org *Email:* info@lamitopsail.org *Visitors welcome?* Yes *Hours:* Contact attraction directly *Admission:* Contact attraction directly *Operated by:* Los Angeles Maritime Institute *NR?* No *NHL?* No *Built:* 1941 *Latitude:* 33.7318 *Longitude:* -118.2782

AMISTAD

Launched in 2000, the schooner Amistad is a museum ship which conducts living history excursions. *Address:* 129 Church St., Suite 521 *City:* New Haven *State:* CT *Zip:* 06510 *Phone:* 203-498-8222 Toll-free: 866-264-7823 *Web:* www.discoveringamistad.org *Email:* info@discoveringamistad.org *Visitors welcome?* Yes *Hours:* Contact attraction directly *Admission:* Contact attraction directly *Operated by:* Amistad America *NR?* No *NHL?* No *Built:* 2000 *Latitude:* 41.3048 *Longitude:* -72.9232

ANGELIQUE

Launched in 1980, the schooner Angelique is an authentic reproduction of classic 19th-century English Channel and North Sea windjammers. *City:* Camden *State:* ME *Zip:* 04843 *Phone:* 800-282-9989 *Web:* www.sailangelique.com *Email:* windjam@sailangelique.com *Visitors welcome?* Yes *Hours:* Contact attraction directly *Admission:* Contact attraction directly *Operated by:* Yankee Packet Company *NR?* No *NHL?* No *Built:* 1980 *Latitude:* 44.2098 *Longitude:* -69.0648

APPLEDORE II

Launched in 1978, the schooner Appledore II is an excursion and sail training vessel. *Address:* 18 Bayview Landing *City:* Camden *State:* ME *Zip:* 04843 *Phone:* 305-509-9047 *Web:* www.appledore2.com *Email:* resdesk@schoonerappledore.com *Visitors welcome?* Yes *Hours:* Contact attraction directly *Admission:* Contact attraction directly *Operated by:* Schooner Appledore *NR?* No *NHL?* No *Built:* 1978 *Latitude:* 44.2098 *Longitude:* -69.0648

APPLEDORE IV

Launched in 1989, the schooner Appledore IV is an excursion and sail training vessel. *Address:* 107 Fifth Street *City:* Bay City *State:* MI *Zip:* 48708 *Phone:* 989-895-5193 *Web:* www.baysailbaycity.org *Email:* info@baysailbaycity.org *Visitors welcome?* Yes *Hours:* Contact attraction directly *Admission:* Contact attraction directly *Operated by:* BaySail – Appledore Tall Ships *NR?* No *NHL?* No *Built:* 1989 *Latitude:* 43.5993 *Longitude:* -83.8899

APPLEDORE V

Launched in 1992, the schooner Appledore V is an excursion and sail training vessel. *Address:* 107 Fifth Street *City:* Bay City *State:* MI *Zip:* 48708 *Phone:* 989-895-5193 *Web:* www.baysailbaycity.org *Email:* info@baysailbaycity.org *Visitors welcome?* Yes *Hours:* Contact attraction directly *Admission:* Contact attraction directly *Operated by:* BaySail *NR?* No *NHL?* No *Built:* 1992 *Latitude:* 43.5993 *Longitude:* -83.8899

AQUIDNECK

The schooner Aquidneck operates as an excursion vessel. *Address:* 32 Bowen's Wharf *City:* Newport *State:* RI *Zip:* 02840 *Phone:* 401-849-3333 *Web:* www.sightsailing.com *Email:* charters@sightsailing.com *Visitors welcome?* Yes *Hours:* Contact attraction directly *Admission:* Contact attraction directly *Operated by:* Sightsailing *NR?* No *NHL?* No *Latitude:* 41.4870 *Longitude:* -71.3159

ARDELLE

The schooner Ardelle is an excursion vessel. *City:* Essex *State:* ME *Phone:* 978-290-7168 *Web:* schooneradelle.com *Email:* info@schoonerardelle.com Visitors welcome: Yes *Hours:* Contact attraction directly *Admission:* Contact attraction directly Operated by Schooner Ardelle *NR?* No NHL: No *Built:* 2016 *Latitude:* 42.6320 *Longitude:* -70.7829

ARGIA

Launched in 1986, the schooner Argia is a day-sailer out of Mystic, Conn. *Address:* 12 Steamboat Wharf *City:* Mystic *State:* CT *Zip:* 06355 *Phone:* 860-536-0416 *Web:* www.argiamystic.com *Visitors welcome?* Yes *Hours:* Contact attraction directly *Admission:* Contact attraction directly *Operated by:* Argia Mystic Cruises *NR?* No *NHL?* No *Built:* 1986 *Latitude:* 41.3562 *Longitude:* -71.9658

BAGHEERA

Launched in 1924, the schooner Bagheera operates as an excursion and sail training vessel. *Address:* Maine State Pier, 56 Commercial St. *City:* Portland *State:* ME *Zip:* 04101 *Phone:* 207-766-2500 Toll-free: 877-246-6637 *Web:* www.portlandschooner.com *Email:* sails@portlandschooner.com *Visitors welcome?* Yes *Hours:* Contact attraction directly *Admission:* Contact attraction directly *Operated by:* Portland Schooner Company **NR? Yes** *NHL?* No *Built:* 1924

Latitude: 43.6577 *Longitude:* -70.2500

BALCLUTHA

Launched in 1886, the three-masted, square-rigged Balclutha is now a museum at the San Francisco Maritime National Historical Park. *Address:* San Francisco Maritime National Historical Park *City:* San Francisco *State:* CA *Zip:* 94123 *Phone:* 415-561-7000 *Web:* www.nps.gov/safr/ *Visitors welcome?* Yes *Hours:* Contact attraction directly *Admission:* $15 *Operated by:* San Francisco Maritime National Historical Park **NR? Yes NHL? Yes** *Built:* 1886 *Latitude:* 37.8097 *Longitude:* -122.4220

BEAVER

The brig Beaver is a replica of an 18th century vessel that played a role in the Boston Tea Party, and serves as a floating exhibit at the Boston Tea Party Ships & Museum. *Address:* 306 Congress St. *City:* Boston *State:* MA *Zip:* 02210 *Phone:* 866-955-0667 *Web:* www.bostonteapartyship.com *Visitors welcome?* Yes *Hours:* 10 a.m. to 4 p.m. directly *Admission:* Contact attraction directly *Operated by:* Historic Tours of America *NR?* No *NHL?* No *Latitude:* 42.3517 *Longitude:* -71.0506

BILL OF RIGHTS

Built in 1971, the Bill of Rights is an educational vessel based in the San Diego area. *Address:* Chula Vista Harbor *City:* Chula Vista *State:* CA *Phone:* 619-500-2419 *Web:* schoonerbillofrights.com *Email:* office@sbfsa.org *Visitors welcome?* Yes *Hours:* Contact attraction directly *Admission:* Contact attraction directly *Operated by:* Los Angeles Maritime Institute *NR?* No *NHL?* No *Built:* 1971 *Latitude:* 32.6239 *Longitude:* -117.0984

BONNIE LYNN

Launched in 1997, the schooner Bonnie Lynn is an excursion vessel. *City:* Islesboro *State:* ME *Zip:* 04848 *Phone:* 401-835-3368 *Web:* www.bonnielynn.com *Email:* mack@bonnielynn.com *Visitors welcome?* Yes *Hours:* Contact attraction directly *Admission:* Contact attraction directly *Operated by:* Schooner Bonnie Lynn *NR?* No *NHL?* No *Built:* 1997 *Latitude:* 44.2957 *Longitude:* -68.9124

BOWDOIN

Launched in 1921, the schooner Bowdoin is a research and education vessel operated by the Maine Maritime Academy. *Address:* 1 Pleasant Street *City:* Castine *State:* ME *Zip:* 04420 *Phone:* 207-326-4311 *Web:* www.mainemaritime.edu *Email:* admissions@mma.edu *Visitors welcome?* Yes *Hours:* Contact attraction directly *Admission:* Contact attraction directly *Operated by:* Maine Maritime Academy **NR? Yes NHL? Yes** *Built:* 1921 *Latitude:* 44.3870 *Longitude:* -68.7980

BRANDARIS

Launched in 1938, the sloop Brandaris is now an excursion and sail training vessel. *Address:* 37 Ocean Ave. *City:* North Kingston *State:* RI *Zip:* 02852 *Phone:* 401-294-0021 *Web:* www.brandarismaritime.com *Email:* info@brandarismaritime.com *Visitors welcome?* Yes *Hours:* Contact attraction directly *Admission:* Contact attraction directly *Operated by:* Brandaris Maritime *NR?* No *NHL?* No *Built:* 1938 *Latitude:* 41.5753 *Longitude:* -71.4497

BRILLIANT

Launched in 1932, the auxiliary gaff schooner Brilliant serves as a sailing training and education vessel at Mystic Seaport Museum. *Address:* 75 Greenmanville Avenue *City:* Mystic *State:* CT *Zip:* 06355 *Phone:* 860-572-0711 *Web:* www.mysticseaport.org *Email:* info@mysticseaport.org *Visitors welcome?* Yes *Hours:* Thursday to Sunday, 10 a.m. to 4 p.m. *Admission:* Adults, $23.95; Seniors, $21.95; Youth 13-17, $19.95; Child 4-12, $16.95 *Operated by:* Mystic Seaport: The Museum of America and the Sea **NR? Yes** *NHL?* No *Built:* 1932 *Latitude:* 41.3617 *Longitude:* -71.9634

C.A. THAYER

Launched in 1895, the three-masted lumber schooner C.A. Thayer is now a museum ship at the San Francisco Maritime National Historical Park. *Address:* San Francisco Maritime National Historical Park *City:* San Francisco *State:* CA *Zip:* 94123 *Phone:* 415-561-7006 *Web:* www.nps.gov/safr/ *Visitors welcome?* Yes *Hours:* Contact attraction directly *Admission:* $15 *Admission:* Contact attraction directly *Operated by:* San Francisco Maritime National Historical Park **NR?**

Yes NHL? Yes Built: 1895 *Latitude:* 37.8070 *Longitude:* -122.4220

CALEB W. JONES

Launched in 1953, the skipjack Caleb W. Jones is privately owned. *City:* Cobb Island *State:* MD *Visitors welcome?* No *Hours:* Contact attraction directly *Admission:* Contact attraction directly *Operated by:* Private owner *NR?* No *NHL?* No *Built:* 1953 *Latitude:* 38.2585 *Longitude:* -76.8439

CALIFORNIAN

Launched in 1984, the Californian is a replica of the cutter C.W. Lawrence, that patrolled the coast of California enforcing federal law during the California Gold Rush. She is an operating vessel that takes passengers on sailing excursions for the San Diego Maritime Museum. *Address:* 1492 North Harbor Drive *City:* San Diego *State:* CA *Zip:* 92101 *Phone:* 619-234-9153 *Web:* www.sdmaritime.com *Email:* support@sdmaritime.org *Visitors welcome?* Yes *Hours:* Daily, 10 a.m. to 8 p.m. *Admission:* $20 18+; $15 seniors, military, students; $10 children three to 12; children under two FREE *Operated by:* Maritime Museum Association of San Diego *NR? Yes NHL? Yes Built:* 1984 *Latitude:* 32.7276 *Longitude:* -117.1800

CAPTAIN EDWARD H. ADAMS

Launched in 1982, the gundalow Captain Edward H. Adams is a museum vessel honoring the maritime history of the Piscataqua River. *Address:* 60 Marcy St. *City:* Portsmouth *State:* NH *Zip:* 03802 *Phone:* 603-433-9505 *Web:* www.gundalow.org *Email:* info@gundalow.org *Visitors welcome?* Yes *Hours:* Contact attraction directly *Admission:* Contact attraction directly *Operated by:* Gundalow Company *NR?* No *NHL?* No *Built:* 1982 *Latitude:* 43.0719 *Longitude:* -70.7632

CHARLES W. MORGAN

Launched in 1841, the barque and whaleship Charles W. Morgan is the premiere floating maritime exhibit at Mystic Seaport. *Address:* 75 Greenmanville Avenue *City:* Mystic *State:* CT *Zip:* 06355 *Phone:* 860-572-0711 *Web:* www.mysticseaport.org *Email:* info@mysticseaport.org *Visitors welcome?* Yes *Hours:* Thursday to

Sunday, 10 a.m. to 4 p.m. *Admission:* $23.95 adults; $21.95 seniors; $19.95 youth 13-17; $16.95 child 4-12 *Operated by:* Mystic Seaport: The Museum of America and the Sea **NR? Yes** NHL? No *Built:* 1841 *Latitude:* 41.3617 *Longitude:* -71.9634

CHRISTEEN

Launched in 1883, the oyster sloop Christeen is an excursion and floating classroom operated by the Waterfront Center. *Address:* 1 West End Ave. *City:* Oyster Bay *State:* NY *Zip:* 11771 *Phone:* 516-922-7245 *Web:* www.thewaterfrontcenter.org *Email:* info@thewaterfrontcenter.org *Visitors welcome?* Yes *Hours:* Contact attraction directly *Admission:* Contact attraction directly *Operated by:* Waterfront Center NR? No **NHL? Yes** *Built:* 1883 *Latitude:* 40.6552 *Longitude:* -73.4775

CITY OF CRISFIELD

Launched in 1949, the skipjack City of Crisfield is privately owned. *City:* Deal Island *State:* MD *Visitors welcome?* No *Operated by:* Private owner NR? No NHL? No *Built:* 1949 *Latitude:* 38.1590 *Longitude:* -75.9480

CLARENCE CROCKETT

Launched in 1908, the skipjack Clarence Crockett is privately owned. *City:* Wenona *State:* MD *Visitors welcome?* No *Operated by:* Private owner **NR? Yes** NHL? No *Built:* 1908 *Latitude:* 38.1390 *Longitude:* -75.9502

CLAUD W. SOMERS

Launched in 1911, the skipjack Claud W. Somers is an operating museum and excursion vessel. *Address:* 504 Main Street *City:* Reedville *State:* VA *Zip:* 22539 *Phone:* 804-453-6529 *Web:* www.rfmuseum.org *Visitors welcome?* Yes *Hours:* Thursday to Saturday, 11 a.m. to 4 p.m. *Admission:* $5 adults, $3 seniors, children 12 and under FREE *Operated by:* Reedville Fisherman's Museum **NR? Yes** NHL? No *Built:* 1911 *Latitude:* 37.8454 *Longitude:* -76.2742

CLEARWATER

Launched in 1969, the Hudson River sloop Clearwater specializes in environmental education activities. *Address:* 724 Wolcott Ave. *City:* Beacon *State:* NY *Zip:* 12508 *Phone:* 845-265 8080 *Web:* www.clearwater.org *Email:* office@clearwater.org *Visitors welcome?* Yes *Hours:* Contact attraction directly *Admission:* Contact attraction directly *Operated by:* Hudson River Sloop Clearwater *NR?* No *NHL?* No *Built:* 1969 *Latitude:* 41.6998 *Longitude:* -73.9316

CORWITH CRAMER

Launched in 1987, the brigantine Corwith Cramer is a sail training and research vessel. *City:* Woods Hole *State:* MA *Zip:* 02543 *Phone:* 508-540-3954 Toll-free: 800-552-3633 *Web:* www.sea.edu *Email:* admission@sea.edu *Visitors welcome?* Yes *Hours:* Contact attraction directly *Admission:* Contact attraction directly *Operated by:* Sea Education Association *NR?* No *NHL?* No *Built:* 1987 *Latitude:* 41.5302 *Longitude:* -70.6603

DEE OF ST. MARY'S

Launched in 1979, the skipjack Dee of St. Mary's conducts environmental education and natural history excursions. *Address:* 14200 Solomons Island Road *City:* Solomons *State:* MD *Zip:* 20688 *Phone:* 410-326-2042 *Web:* www.calvertmarinemuseum.com *Email:* Kathleen.Porecki@calvertcountymd.gov *Visitors welcome?* Yes *Hours:* Contact attraction directly *Admission:* Contact attraction directly *Operated by:* Calvert Maritime Museum *NR?* No *NHL?* No *Built:* 1979 *Latitude:* 38.3310 *Longitude:* -76.4643

DENIS SULLIVAN

Launched in 2000, the schooner Denis Sullivan is a sailing training, goodwill ambassador, and education vessel. *Address:* 500 N. Harbor Dr. *City:* Milwaukee *State:* WI *Zip:* 53202 *Phone:* 414-765-9966 *Web:* www.discoveryworld.org *Email:* info@discoveryworld.org *Visitors welcome?* Yes *Hours:* Contact attraction directly *Admission:* $20 adults, $16 seniors, children 3-17; $14 college student, active military; under two FREE *Operated by:* Discovery World *NR?* No *NHL?* No *Built:* 2000 *Latitude:* 43.0331 *Longitude:* -87.8997

DILIGENCE

Completed in 2016, the replica of the schooner Diligence is a permanent exhibit at Independence Seaport Museum. *Address:* 211 South Columbus Blvd. *City:* Philadelphia *State:* PA *Zip:* 19106 *Phone:* 215-413-8655 *Web:* www.phillyseaport.org *Email:* seaport@phillyseaport.org *Visitors welcome?* Yes *Hours:* Thursday to Saturday, 10 a.m. to 5 p.m., Sunday, noon to 5 p.m. *Admission:* $18 adults; $10 seniors; $14 children, seniors, military; children under two FREE *Operated by:* Independence Seaport Museum **NR? Yes NHL? Yes** *Built:* 2016 *Latitude:* 39.9457 *Longitude:* -75.1419

DISCOVERY

Launched in 2007, the Discovery is a working replica of a ship that brought the first colonists to the Jamestown settlement. *Address:* 2218 Jamestown Rd. *City:* Williamsburg *State:* VA *Zip:* 23185 *Phone:* 757-253-7308 *Web:* historyisfun.org *Visitors welcome?* Yes *Hours:* Daily, 10 a.m. to 4:30 p.m *Admission:* Contact attraction directly *Operated by:* Jamestown-Yorktown Foundation *NR?* No *NHL?* No *Built:* 2007 *Latitude:* 37.2251 *Longitude:* -76.7862

Many tall ships offer opportunities for you to learn how to sail. Ask a crew member about its sail training program.

DOROTHY A. PARSONS

The 84-foot Dorothy A. Parsons is on display at the northern campus of the Piney Point Lighthouse Museum. *Address:* 44720 Lighthouse Road *City:* Piney Point *State:* MD *Zip:* 20674 *Phone:* 301-994-1471 *Web:* www.stmarysmd.com/recreate/Museums *Visitors welcome?* Yes *Hours:* March 25 to October 31, Daily, 10 a.m. to 5 p.m. *Admission:* $7 adults, $3.50 seniors/students/active military, children under five FREE *Operated by:* St. Mary's County Museum Division *NR?* No *NHL?* No *Latitude:* 38.1408 *Longitude:* -76.5202

DREAM CATCHER

Launched in 1996, the schooner Dream Catcher is a sailing training and excursion vessel. *Address:* 28555 Jolly Roger Dr. *City:* Little Torch Key *State:* FL *Zip:* 33042 *Phone:* 305-304-5100 *Web:* islandsailingadventure.com *Email:* islandsailingadventure@gmail.com *Visitors welcome?* Yes *Hours:* Contact attraction directly *Admission:* Contact attraction directly *Operated by:* Island Sailing Adventures *NR?* No *NHL?* No *Built:* 1996 *Latitude:* 24.6546 *Longitude:* -81.3863

E.C. COLLIER

Launched in 1910, the skipjack E.C. Collier is a dry-berth exhibit at the Chesapeake Bay Maritime Museum. *Address:* 213 N. Talbot Street *City:* St. Michaels *State:* MD *Zip:* 21663 *Phone:* 410-745-2916 *Web:* www.cbmm.org *Email:* havefun@cbmm.org *Visitors welcome?* Yes *Hours:* Daily, hours vary by season *Admission:* $16 adults; $13 seniors over 62, students; $12 retired military; $6 kids 6 to 17; active military, kids under 6 FREE *Operated by:* Chesapeake Bay Maritime Museum **NR? Yes** NHL? No *Built:* 1910 *Latitude:* 38.7876 *Longitude:* -76.2249

EDNA E. LOCKWOOD

The Edna E. Lockwood is the last sailing log-bottom bugeye. A bugeye's hull is constructed by pinning together a series of logs and hollowing them out as a unit. *Address:* 213 N. Talbot Street *City:* St. Michaels *State:* MD *Zip:* 21663 *Phone:* 410-745-2916 *Web:* www.cbmm.org *Email:* havefun@cbmm.org *Visitors welcome?* Yes *Hours:* Daily, hours vary by season *Admission:* $16 adults; $13 seniors over 62, students; $12 retired military; $6 kids 6 to 17; active military, kids under 6 FREE *Operated by:* Chesapeake Bay Maritime Museum NR? No NHL? No *Built:* 1910 *Latitude:* 38.7876 *Longitude:* -76.2249

ELISSA

Launched in 1877, the iron-hulled barque Elissa is the premier operating exhibit at the Texas Seaport Museum. *Address:* 2200 Harborside *City:* Galveston *State:* TX *Zip:* 77550 *Phone:* 409-763-1877 *Web:* www.tsm-elissa.org *Email:* elissa@galvestonhistory.org *Visitors welcome?* Yes *Hours:* Daily, 10 a.m. to 5 p.m. *Admission:* $6 adults, $4.50 students six through 18, children five and under FREE *Operated by:* Galveston Historical Foundation **NR? Yes NHL? Yes** *Built:* 1877 *Latitude:* 29.3263 *Longitude:* -94.7951

ELIZABETH II

Launched in 1983, the barque Elizabeth II is a replica of a typical 16th century vessel that sailed between England and America. It is now used as a sail training and living history classroom. *Address:* One Festival Park *City:* Manteo *State:* NC *Zip:* 27954 *Phone:* 252-475-1500 *Web:* www.roanokeisland.com *Email:*

festivalparkinformation@ncdcr.gov *Visitors welcome?* Yes *Hours:*
Contact attraction directly *Admission:* Contact attraction directly
Operated by: Roanoke Island Festival Park *NR?* No *NHL?* No *Built:*
1983 *Latitude:* 35.9113 *Longitude:* -75.6673

ELSWORTH

Launched in 1901, the skipjack Elsworth is now operated by an
outdoor school for youth. *Address:* 13655 Bloomingneck Road *City:*
Worton *State:* MD *Zip:* 21678 *Phone:* 410-348-5880 *Web:*
www.ehos.org *Email:* info@ehos.org *Visitors welcome?* Yes *Hours:*
Contact attraction directly *Admission:* Contact attraction directly
Operated by: Echo Hill Outdoor School *NR?* No *NHL?* No *Built:*
1901 *Latitude:* 39.3554 *Longitude:* -76.1130

ELVA C

Launched in 1922, the deck boat Elva C. is an operating museum and
excursion vessel. *Address:* 504 Main Street *City:* Reedville *State:* VA
Zip: 22539 *Phone:* 804-453-6529 *Web:* www.rfmuseum.org *Visitors
welcome?* Yes *Hours:* Thursday to Saturday, 11 a.m. to 4 p.m. *Admission:*
$5 adults, $3 seniors, children 12 and under FREE *Operated by:*
Reedville Fisherman's Museum **NR? Yes** NHL? No *Built:* 1922
Latitude: 37.8454 *Longitude:* -76.2742

EMMA C. BERRY

Launched in 1866, the sloop Emma C. Berry is now part of the
Mystic Seaport ship collection. *Address:* 75 Greenmanville Avenue
City: Mystic *State:* CT *Zip:* 06355 *Phone:* 860-572-0711 *Web:*
www.mysticseaport.org *Email:* info@mysticseaport.org *Visitors
welcome?* Yes *Hours:* Thursday to Sunday, 10 a.m. to 4 p.m. *Admission:*
$23.95 adults; $21.95 seniors; $19.95 youth 13-17; $16.95 child 4-12
Operated by: Mystic Seaport: The Museum of America and the Sea
NR? Yes NHL? No *Built:* 1866 *Latitude:* 41.3617 *Longitude:* -71.9634

EQUATOR

Launched in 1888, the schooner Equator is now a covered dry-berth
exhibit at the Port of Everett. *Address:* W. Marine View Dr. and 10th
St. *City:* Everett *State:* WA *Visitors welcome?* Yes *Hours:* Daily *Admission:*
FREE **NR? Yes** NHL? No *Built:* 1888 *Latitude:* 48.0043 *Longitude:* -

122.2140

ERNESTINA-MORRISSEY

Launched in 1894, the fishing schooner Ernestina-Morrissey is now an operational sail training vessel. *Address:* 101 Academy Drive *City:* Buzzards Bay *State:* MA *Zip:* 02532 *Phone:* 508-830-5000 *Web:* ernestina.org *Email:* admissions@maritime.edu *Visitors welcome?* Yes *Hours:* Contact attraction directly *Admission:* Contact attraction directly *Operated by:* Massachusetts Maritime Academy Commission *NR? Yes NHL? Yes Built:* 1894 *Latitude:* 41.7408 *Longitude:* -70.6223

EVELINA M. GOULART

Launched in 1927, the fishing schooner Evelina M. Goulart is undergoing preservation and documentation at the Essex Shipbuilding Museum. *Address:* 66 Main Street *City:* Essex *State:* MA *Zip:* 01929 *Phone:* 978-768-7541 *Web:* www.essexshipbuildingmuseum.org *Email:* office@essexshipbuildingmuseum.org *Visitors welcome?* Yes *Hours:* Contact attraction directly *Admission:* Contact attraction directly *Operated by:* Essex Historical Society & Shipbuilding Museum *NR?* No *NHL?* No *Built:* 1927 *Latitude:* 42.6323 *Longitude:* -70.7795

EXY JOHNSON

Completed in 2003, the Exy Johnson was purpose-designed to meet the specific needs of LAMI's TopSail Youth Program. One of twin brigantines, this state-of-the-art sail training vessel joins Irving Johnson as the flag ship of the LAMI fleet. *Address:* Berth 73, Suite 2 *City:* San Pedro *State:* CA *Phone:* 310-833-6055 *Web:* lamitopsail.org *Email:* info@lamitopsail.org *Visitors welcome?* Yes *Hours:* Contact attraction directly *Admission:* Contact attraction directly *Operated by:* Los Angeles Maritime Institute *NR?* No *NHL?* No *Built:* 2003 *Latitude:* 33.7387 *Longitude:* -118.2790

F.C. LEWIS, JR.

Launched in 1907, the skipjack F.C. Lewis, Jr. is a dry-berth exhibit at the Choptank River Heritage Center. *Address:* 10215 River Landing Rd. *City:* West Denton *State:* MI *Zip:* 21629 *Phone:* 410-479-4150 *Web:* choptankriverheritage.org *Email:* carolinemdhistory@gmail.com

Visitors welcome? Yes *Hours:* May to September: Friday and Saturday, 11 a.m. to 3 p.m. *Admission:* Contact attraction directly *Operated by:* Choptank River Heritage Center **NR? Yes** *NHL?* No *Built:* 1907 *Latitude:* 38.8881 *Longitude:* -75.8399

FAITH

Launched in 1968, the skipjack Faith (formerly Ada Fears) is an operating oyster dredger. *City:* Deal Island *State:* MD *Visitors welcome?* No *Hours:* None *Admission:* None *Operated by:* Private owner *NR?* No *NHL?* No *Built:* 1968 *Latitude:* 39.1590 *Longitude:* -76.9480

FALLS OF CLYDE

Launched in 1878, Falls of Clyde is the only surviving iron-hulled four-masted full rigged ship and the only surviving sail-driven oil tanker in the world. She is currently berthed at Honolulu Harbor with a plan to return her to Scotland, where she was built. *Address:* Pier 7 *City:* Honolulu *State:* HI *Zip:* 96813 *Phone:* 808-479-0702 *Web:* www.friendsoffallsofclyde.org *Email:* bemacewan@gmail.com *Visitors welcome?* Yes *Operated by:* Friends of Falls of Clyde **NR? Yes NHL? Yes** *Built:* 1878 *Latitude:* 21.3165 *Longitude:* -157.8890

FAME OF SALEM

The schooner Fame of Salem is a replica of the original Fame, a fast Chebacco fishing schooner that was reborn as a privateer when war broke out in the summer of 1812. *Address:* 86 Wharf Street *City:* Salem *State:* MA *Zip:* 01970 *Phone:* 978-729-7600 *Web:* www.schoonerfame.com *Email:* SchoonerFame@gmail.com *Visitors welcome?* Yes *Hours:* Daily, Memorial Day through Halloween *Admission:* Contact attraction directly *Operated by:* Pennant Enterprises *NR?* No *NHL?* No *Built:* 2003 *Latitude:* 42.5207 *Longitude:* -70.8901

FANNIE L. DAUGHERTY

Launched in 1904, the skipjack Fannie L. Daugherty was recently restored by the Chesapeake Bay Maritime Museum. *City:* Deal Island *State:* MD *Visitors welcome?* No *Operated by:* Private owner *NR?* No *NHL?* No *Built:* 1904 *Latitude:* 38.1590 *Longitude:* -75.9480

FLORA A. PRICE

The skipjack Flora A. Price is the largest surviving Chesapeake Bay skipjack, and it is used a floating classroom by the Choptank River Heritage Center. *Address:* 10215 River Landing Rd. *City:* West Denton *State:* MI *Zip:* 21629 *Phone:* 410-479-4150 *Web:* choptankriverheritage.org *Email:* carolinemdhistory@gmail.com *Visitors welcome?* Yes *Hours:* May to September: Friday and Saturday, 11 a.m. to 3 p.m. *Admission:* Contact attraction directly *Operated by:* Choptank River Heritage Center *NR?* No *NHL?* No *Latitude:* 38.8881 *Longitude:* -75.8399

FRIENDS GOOD WILL

Friends Good Will is a reproduction of a sloop that participated in the 1812 Battle of Lake Erie. *Address:* 260 Dyckman Ave. *City:* South Haven *State:* MI *Zip:* 49090 *Phone:* 269-637-8078 *Web:* michiganmaritimemuseum.org *Visitors welcome?* Yes *Hours:* Memorial Day to Labor Day: Daily, 10 a.m. to 5 p.m. *Admission:* $8 adults; $7 seniors, veterans, active military; $5 children; under four FREE *Operated by:* Michigan Maritime Museum *NR?* No *NHL?* No *Built:* 2004 *Latitude:* 42.4070 *Longitude:* -86.2745

FRIENDSHIP

The East Indiaman Friendship is a replica of the original vessel launched in 1797. She made 15 voyages during her career to Batavia, India, China, South America, the Caribbean, England, Germany, the Mediterranean, and Russia. *Address:* 2 New Liberty Street *City:* Salem *State:* MA *Zip:* 01970 *Phone:* 978-740-1650 *Web:* www.nps.gov/sama/ *Email:* colleen_bruce@nps.gov *Visitors welcome?* Yes *Hours:* Daily, 9 a.m. to 5 p.m. *Admission:* $15 adults *Operated by:* Salem National Maritime Historic Site *NR?* No *NHL?* No *Built:* 1996 *Latitude:* 42.5227 *Longitude:* -70.8920

FRITHA

Launched in 1985, the brigantine Fritha is a sail training and education vessel. *Address:* 32 Washington St. *City:* Fairhaven *State:* MA *Zip:* 02719 *Phone:* 508-992-4025 *Web:* www.northeastmaritime.com *Email:* admissions@northeastmaritime.com *Visitors welcome?* Yes *Hours:*

Monday through Friday 8 a.m. to 5 p.m. *Admission:* Contact attraction directly *Operated by:* Northeast Maritime Institute *NR?* No *NHL?* No *Built:* 1985 *Latitude:* 41.6374 *Longitude:* -70.9034

GAZELA PRIMEIRO

Launched in 1883, the barkentine Gazela Primiero is a fishing vessel converted to a working museum ship. *Address:* Foot of Market Street *City:* Philadelphia *State:* PA *Zip:* 19106 *Phone:* 215-238-0280 *Web:* www.gazela.org *Email:* office@philashipguild.org *Visitors welcome?* Yes *Hours:* Contact attraction directly *Admission:* Contact attraction directly *Operated by:* Philadelphia Ship Preservation Guild *NR?* No *NHL?* No *Built:* 1883 *Latitude:* 39.9505 *Longitude:* -75.1481

GLENN L. SWETMAN

The Maritime & Seafood Industry Museum in Biloxi, Miss., has recaptured a piece of its history with their two schooners, the Glenn L. Swetman and the Mike Sekul. Available for day sailing or charter, the vessels can accommodate weddings, dockside parties, and other functions. *Address:* 115 First Street *City:* Biloxi *State:* MS *Zip:* 39530 *Phone:* 228-435-6320 *Web:* www.maritimemuseum.org *Email:* info@maritimemuseum.org *Visitors welcome?* Yes *Hours:* Monday through Saturday, 9 a.m. to 4:30 p.m.; Sunday, noon to 4 p.m. *Admission:* $10 adults; $8 seniors, active military; $6 students 5-15 *Operated by:* Maritime & Seafood Industry Museum *NR?* No *NHL?* No *Latitude:* 30.3937 *Longitude:* -88.8591

GODSPEED

Launched in 2006, the Godspeed is a working replica of a ship that brought the first colonists to the Jamestown settlement. *Address:* 2218 Jamestown Rd. *City:* Williamsburg *State:* VA *Zip:* 23185 *Phone:* 757-253-7308 *Web:* historyisfun.org *Visitors welcome?* Yes *Hours:* Daily, 10 a.m. to 4:30 p.m. *Admission:* Contact attraction directly *Operated by:* Jamestown-Yorktown Foundation *NR?* No *NHL?* No *Built:* 2006 *Latitude:* 37.2251 *Longitude:* -76.7862

GOVERNOR STONE

Launched in 1877, the schooner Governor Stone is the last surviving Gulf schooner cargo vessel. It is now undergoing restoration. *City:*

Fort Walton Beach *State:* FL *Zip:* 32549 *Phone:* 850-621-0011 *Web:* www.governorstone.org *Email:* info@governorstone.org *Visitors welcome?* Yes *Hours:* Contact attraction directly *Admission:* Contact attraction directly *Operated by:* Friends of the Governor Stone *NR?* No **NHL? Yes** *Built:* 1877 *Latitude:* 30.4057 *Longitude:* -86.6188

The latitude and longitude noted in each listing is approximate and based on publicly available data. Always visit the vessel's website or call to get the exact location, such a pier or berth number.

GRACE BAILEY

Launched in 1882, the schooner Grace Bailey is now an excursion vessel. *Address:* Camden Waterfront *City:* Camden *State:* ME *Zip:* 04843 *Phone:* 207-236-2938 Toll-free: 800-736-7981 *Web:* www.mainewindjammercruises.com *Email:* sail@mainewindjammercruises.com *Visitors welcome?* Yes *Hours:* Contact attraction directly *Admission:* Contact attraction directly *Operated by:* Maine Windjammer Cruises **NR? Yes NHL? Yes** *Built:* 1882 *Latitude:* 44.2098 *Longitude:* -69.0648

GRACIE L

Launched in 1982, the Mackinaw boat Gracie L. is a sailing training and education vessel. *Address:* 13268 S. West Bayshore Dr *City:* Traverse City *State:* MI *Zip:* 49684 *Phone:* 231-946-2647 *Web:* www.maritimeheritagealliance.org *Email:* mark@maritimeheritagealliance.org *Visitors welcome?* Yes *Hours:* Contact attraction directly *Admission:* Contact attraction directly *Operated by:* Maritime Heritage Alliance *NR?* No *NHL?* No *Built:* 1982 *Latitude:* 44.7617 *Longitude:* -85.6266

H.M. KRENTZ

Launched in 1955, the skipjack H.M. Krentz is an excursion vessel. *City:* St. Michaels *State:* MD *Zip:* 21663 *Phone:* 410-745-6080 *Web:* www.oystercatcher.com *Email:* capted55@gmail.com *Visitors welcome?* Yes *Hours:* Contact attraction directly *Admission:* Contact attraction directly *Operated by:* Skipjack H.M. Krentz *NR?* No *NHL?* No *Built:* 1955 *Latitude:* 38.7827 *Longitude:* -76.2363

HAILE & MATTHEW

The schooner Haile & Matthew is an excursion vessel operating out of Portland, Maine. *City:* Portland ME *Email:* svhaliematthew@gmail.com *Visitors welcome?* Yes *NR?* No *NHL?* No *Built:* 2005 *Latitude:* 43.6630 *Longitude:* -70.2569

HALF MOON

The Half Moon is a reproduction of the ship that Henry Hudson sailed from Holland to the New World in 1609. *Address:* 181 S Riverside Ave. *City:* Croton-on-Hudson *State:* NY *Zip:* 10520 *Phone:* 518-443-1609 *Web:* www.newnetherlandmuseum.org *Email:* info@newnetherlandmuseum.org *Visitors welcome?* Yes *Hours:* Contact attraction directly *Admission:* Contact attraction directly *Operated by:* New Netherland Museum & Half Moon Visitor's Center *NR?* No *NHL?* No *Latitude:* 41.2024 *Longitude:* -73.8875

HARVEY GAMAGE

Launched in 1973, the schooner Harvey Gamage is a sailing training vessel. *City:* Portland *State:* ME *Phone:* 207-405-8485 *Web:* sailingshipsmaine.org *Email:* info@sailingshipsmaine.org *Visitors welcome?* Yes *Hours:* Contact attraction directly *Admission:* Contact attraction directly *Operated by:* Sailing Ships Maine *NR?* No *NHL?* No *Built:* 1973 *Latitude:* 43.6630 *Longitude:* -70.2569

HAWAIIAN CHIEFTAIN

Launched in 1988, the topsail ketch Hawaiian Chieftain is an excursion and sail training vessel. *State:* HI *Visitors welcome?* No *Hours:* Contact attraction directly *Admission:* Contact attraction directly *Operated by:* Private owner *NR?* No *NHL?* No *Built:* 1988

HELEN VIRGINIA

Launched in 1948, the skipjack Helen Virginia is working oyster dredger on Chesapeake Bay. *City:* Deal Island: MD *Visitors welcome?* No *Hours:* Contact attraction directly *Admission:* Contact attraction directly *Operated by:* Skipjack Helen Virginia **NR? Yes** *NHL?* No *Built:* 1948 *Latitude:* 38.1590 *Longitude:* -75.9480

HERITAGE

Launched in 1983, the schooner Heritage was constructed along the traditional lines of the schooners that navigated the waters off the coast of Maine more than a hundred years ago. *Address:* 5 Achorn Street *City:* Rockland *State:* ME *Zip:* 04841 *Phone:* 207-594-8007 Toll-free: 800-648-4544 *Web:* www.schoonerheritage.com *Email:* info@schoonerheritage.com *Visitors welcome?* Yes *Hours:* Contact attraction directly *Admission:* Contact attraction directly *Operated by:* Schooner Heritage *NR?* No *NHL?* No *Built:* 1983 *Latitude:* 44.1127 *Longitude:* -69.1049

HERITAGE OF MIAMI II

Launched in 1988, the schooner Heritage of Miami II is a sail training and excursion vessel. *Address:* 3145 Virginia St. *City:* Coconut Grove *State:* FL *Zip:* 33133 *Phone:* 305-442-9697 *Web:* www.heritageschooner.com *Email:* heritage2@mindspring.com *Visitors welcome?* Yes *Hours:* Contact attraction directly *Admission:* Contact attraction directly *Operated by:* Heritage Schooner Cruises *NR?* No *NHL?* No *Built:* 1988 *Latitude:* 25.7328 *Longitude:* -80.2414

HIGHLANDER SEA

Launched in 1924, the schooner Highlander Sea is an excursion and sail training vessel. *City:* Port Huron *State:* MI *Zip:* 48060 *Phone:* 810-966-3488 *Email:* caphighlandersea@achesonventures.com *Visitors welcome?* Yes *Hours:* Contact attraction directly *Admission:* Contact attraction directly *Operated by:* Acheson Ventures *NR?* No *NHL?* No *Built:* 1924 *Latitude:* 42.9591 *Longitude:* -82.4274

HILDA M. WILLING

Launched in 1905, the skipjack Hilda M. Willing is a working vessel on Chesapeake Bay. *City:* Tilghman Island *State:* MD *Visitors welcome?* No *Operated by:* Private owner **NR? Yes NHL? Yes** *Built:* 1905 *Latitude:* 38.7037 *Longitude:* -76.3386

HOWARD

Launched in 1909, the skipjack Howard is a working vessel on Chesapeake Bay. *City:* Wenona *State:* MD *Visitors welcome?* No *Operated by:* Private owner **NR? Yes** *NHL?* No *Built:* 1909 *Latitude:* 38.1390

Longitude: -75.9502

IDA MAY

Launched in 1906, the skipjack Ida May is a working vessel on Chesapeake Bay. *City:* Deal Island *State:* MD *Visitors welcome?* No *Operated by:* Private owner **NR? Yes** NHL? No *Built:* 1906 *Latitude:* 38.1590 *Longitude:* -75.9480

INLAND SEAS

Launched in 1994, the schooner Inland Seas is a sailing training and maritime education vessel. *Address:* 100 Dame St. *City:* Suttons Bay *State:* MI *Zip:* 49682 *Phone:* 231-271-3077 *Web:* www.schoolship.org *Email:* isea@schoolship.org *Visitors welcome?* Yes *Hours:* Monday through Friday, 8:30 a.m. to 5 p.m. *Admission:* Contact attraction directly *Operated by:* Inland Seas Education Association *NR?* No *NHL?* No *Built:* 1994 *Latitude:* 44.9750 *Longitude:* -85.6497

IRVING JOHNSON

Completed in 2003, the Irving Johnson was purpose-designed to meet the specific needs of LAMI's TopSail Youth Program. One of twin brigantines, this state-of-the-art sail training vessel joins Exy Johnson as the flag ship of the LAMI fleet. *Address:* Berth 84, Foot of 6th St. *City:* San Pedro *State:* CA *Zip:* 90731 *Phone:* 310-833-6055 *Web:* www.lamitopsail.org *Email:* info@lamitopsail.org *Visitors welcome?* Yes *Hours:* Contact attraction directly *Admission:* Contact attraction directly *Operated by:* Los Angeles Maritime Institute *NR?* No *NHL?* No *Built:* 2003 *Latitude:* 33.7387 *Longitude:* -118.2790

ISAAC H. EVANS

Launched in 1886, the schooner Isaac H. Evans is now an excursion vessel. *City:* Rockland *State:* ME *Zip:* 04841 *Phone:* 877-238-1325 *Visitors welcome?* Yes *Hours:* Contact attraction directly *Admission:* Contact attraction directly *Operated by:* Schooner Isaac H. Evans **NR? Yes NHL? Yes** *Built:* 1886 *Latitude:* 44.1037 *Longitude:* -69.1089

J. & E. RIGGIN

Launched in 1927, the schooner J. & E. Riggin is now an excursion and cruise vessel. *Address:* 64 Old County Road *City:* Rockland *State:*

ME *Zip:* 04841 *Phone:* 207-594-1875 Toll-free: 800-869-0604 *Web:* www.mainewindjammer.com *Email:* sail@SchoonerRiggin.com *Visitors welcome?* Yes *Hours:* Contact attraction directly *Admission:* Contact attraction directly *Operated by:* Schooner J. & E. Riggin **NR?** **Yes NHL?** **Yes** *Built:* 1927 *Latitude:* 44.0966 *Longitude:* -69.1171

JOSEPH CONRAD

Launched in 1882, the ship Joseph Conrad is a floating exhibit and training vessel at Mystic Seaport. *Address:* 75 Greenmanville Avenue *City:* Mystic *State:* CT *Zip:* 06355 *Phone:* 860-572-0711 *Web:* www.mysticseaport.org *Email:* info@mysticseaport.org *Visitors welcome?* Yes *Hours:* Thursday to Sunday, 10 a.m. to 4 p.m. *Admission:* $23.95 adults; $21.95 seniors; $19.95 youth 13-17; $16.95 child 4-12 *Operated by:* Mystic Seaport: The Museum of America and the Sea **NR? Yes** *NHL?* No *Built:* 1882 *Latitude:* 41.3617 *Longitude:* -71.9634

JOY PARKS

The 64-foot skipjack Joy Parks is on display at the northern campus of the Piney Point Lighthouse Museum. *Address:* 44720 Lighthouse Road *City:* Piney Point *State:* MD *Zip:* 20674 *Phone:* 301-994-1471 *Web:* www.stmarysmd.com/recreate/Museums *Visitors welcome?* Yes *Hours:* March 25 to October 31, Daily, 10 a.m. to 5 p.m. *Admission:* $7 adults, $3.50 seniors/students/active military, children under five FREE *Operated by:* St. Mary's County Museum Division *NR?* No *NHL?* No *Latitude:* 38.1408 *Longitude:* -76.5202

KALMAR NYCKEL

Launched in 1998, the replica Kalmar Nyckel is Delaware's goodwill ambassador and a catalyst for social and economic development. *Address:* 1124 E. Seventh St. *City:* Wilmington *State:* DE *Zip:* 19801 *Phone:* 302-429-7447 *Web:* www.kalmarnyckel.org *Email:* info@kalmarnyckel.org *Visitors welcome?* Yes *Hours:* Contact attraction directly *Admission:* Contact attraction directly *Operated by:* Kalmar Nyckel Foundation *NR?* No *NHL?* No *Built:* 1998 *Latitude:* 39.7377 *Longitude:* -75.5367

KATHRYN

The skipjack Kathryn is a privately operated dredge boat on

Chesapeake Bay. *Address:* Tilghman Island *City:* Tilghman *State:* MD *Visitors welcome?* No *Operated by:* Private owner *NR?* No **NHL? Yes** *Built:* 1901 *Latitude:* 38.7171 *Longitude:* -76.3344

In some cases, visitors may need to walk a significant distance in a marina or waterfront to visit a ship. Always dress appropriately for the weather, and carry plenty of water.

L.A. DUNTON

Launched in 1921, the schooner L.A. Dunton is a floating exhibit at Mystic Seaport. *Address:* 75 Greenmanville Avenue *City:* Mystic *State:* CT *Zip:* 06355 *Phone:* 860-572-0711 *Web:* www.mysticseaport.org *Email:* info@mysticseaport.org *Visitors welcome?* Yes *Hours:* Thursday to Sunday, 10 a.m. to 4 p.m. *Admission:* $23.95 adults; $21.95 seniors; $19.95 youth 13-17; $16.95 child 4-12 *Operated by:* Mystic Seaport: The Museum of America and the Sea **NR? Yes NHL? Yes** *Built:* 1921 *Latitude:* 41.3617 *Longitude:* -71.9634

LADY KATIE

Launched in 1956, the skipjack Lady Katie is a working vessel on Chesapeake Bay. *City:* Cambridge *State:* MD *Visitors welcome?* No *Operated by:* Private owner *NR?* No *NHL?* No *Built:* 1956 *Latitude:* 38.5632 *Longitude:* -76.0788

LADY MARYLAND

Launched in 1986, the schooner Lady Maryland is a sail training and excursion vessel. *Address:* 1417 Thames Street *City:* Baltimore *State:* MD *Zip:* 21231 *Phone:* 410-685-0295 *Web:* www.livingclassrooms.org *Visitors welcome?* Yes *Hours:* Contact attraction directly *Admission:* Contact attraction directly *Operated by:* Living Classrooms Foundation *NR?* No *NHL?* No *Built:* 1986 *Latitude:* 39.2864 *Longitude:* -76.6056

LADY WASHINGTON

Launched in 1989, the brig Lady Washington is a replica of the first American-flagged ship to sail to the west coast of North America. *Address:* 500 N Custer St. *City:* Aberdeen *State:* WA *Zip:* 98520 *Phone:* 360-532-8611 *Web:* historicalseaport.org *Visitors welcome?* Yes *Hours:* Contact attraction directly *Admission:* Contact attraction directly

Operated by: Grays Harbor Historical Seaport Authority *NR?* No
NHL? No *Built:* 1989 *Latitude:* 46.9685 *Longitude:* -123.7730

LAVENGRO

Launched in 1927, the schooner Lavengro is now an excursion and
sail training vessel. *Address:* N. Northlake Way and N. Northlake Pl
City: Seattle *State:* WA *Phone:* 360-399-6490 *Web:*
lakeunioncharters.com *Email:* info@lakeunioncharters.com *Visitors
welcome?* Yes *Hours:* Contact attraction directly *Admission:* Contact
attraction directly *Operated by:* Northwest Schooner Society *NR?* No
NHL? No *Built:* 1927 *Latitude:* 47.6470 *Longitude:* -122.3380

LETTIE G. HOWARD

Launched in 1893, the Lettie G. Howard is a floating exhibit at the
South Street Seaport Museum. *Address:* 12 Fulton St. *City:* New York
State: NY *Zip:* 10038 *Phone:* 212-748-8600 *Web:*
www.southstreetseaportmuseum.org *Email:* info@southstseaport.org
Visitors welcome? Yes *Hours:* Contact attraction directly *Admission:*
Contact attraction directly *Operated by:* South Street Seaport Museum
NR? Yes NHL? Yes *Built:* 1893 *Latitude:* 40.7066 *Longitude:* -74.0034

LEWIS R. FRENCH

Launched in 1871, the schooner Lewis R. French is now an excursion
vessel. *Address:* 11 Atlantic Ave. *City:* Camden *State:* ME *Zip:* 04843
Phone: 207-230-8320 *Toll-free:* 800-469-4635 *Web:*
www.schoonerfrench.com *Email:* captain@schoonerfrench.com
Visitors welcome? Yes *Hours:* Contact attraction directly *Admission:*
Contact attraction directly *Operated by:* Schooner Lewis R. French
NR? Yes NHL? Yes *Built:* 1871 *Latitude:* 44.2098 *Longitude:* -69.0648

LIBERTY CLIPPER

Launched in 1983, the schooner Liberty Clipper is a sail training and
excursion vessel. *Address:* 67 Long Wharf *City:* Boston *State:* MA *Zip:*
02110 *Phone:* 617-742-0333 *Web:* www.libertyfleet.com *Email:*
liberty@libertyfleet.com *Visitors welcome?* Yes *Hours:* Contact
attraction directly *Admission:* Contact attraction directly *Operated by:*
Liberty Fleet *NR?* No *NHL?* No *Built:* 1983 *Latitude:* 42.3608
Longitude: -71.0501

LIBERTY SCHOONER

Launched in 1993, the schooner Liberty Schooner is an excursion and sail training vessel. The schooner winters in Miami Beach, Fla. *Address:* 80 Audrey Zapp Drive *City:* Jersey City *State:* NJ *Zip:* 07305 *Phone:* 973-309-1884 *Web:* www.libertyschooner.com *Email:* liberty.schooner@gmail.com *Visitors welcome?* Yes *Hours:* Contact attraction directly *Admission:* Contact attraction directly *Operated by:* Liberty Schooner *NR?* No *NHL?* No *Built:* 1993 *Latitude:* 40.7094 *Longitude:* -74.0478

LOIS MCCLURE

The schooner Lois McClure is a modern replica of an 1862 sailing canal boat developed for the growing water trade on the region's network of canals. *Address:* 4472 Basin Harbor Rd. *City:* Vergennes *State:* VT *Zip:* 05491 *Phone:* 802-475-2022 *Web:* www.lcmm.org *Email:* info@lcmm.org *Visitors welcome?* Yes *Hours:* Daily, 10 a.m. to 4 p.m. *Admission:* All ages, FREE *Operated by:* Lake Champlain Maritime Museum *NR?* No *NHL?* No *Built:* 2004 *Latitude:* 44.1973 *Longitude:* -73.3567

LOTUS (SCHOONER)

Launched in 1917, the bald-headed gaff auxiliary schooner Lotus is operated by the Sea Scouts. *City:* Webster *State:* NY *Zip:* 14580 *Phone:* 585-244-4210 *Web:* ithilien.mine.nu/lotus/ *Email:* info@senecawaterways.org *Visitors welcome?* Yes *Hours:* Contact attraction directly *Admission:* Contact attraction directly *Operated by:* Seneca Waterways Council **NR? Yes** NHL? No *Built:* 1917 *Latitude:* 43.2123 *Longitude:* -77.4300

LYNX

Launched in 2001, the schooner Lynx is a sailing training and education vessel. *City:* Nantucket *State:* MA *Zip:* 02554 *Phone:* 978-479-2197 *Web:* tallshiplynx.com *Email:* peacock@tallshiplynx.com *Visitors welcome?* Yes *Hours:* Contact attraction directly *Admission:* Contact attraction directly *Operated by:* Egan Maritime Institute *NR?* No *NHL?* No *Built:* 2001 *Latitude:* 33.6142 *Longitude:* -117.9280

MADELINE

Launched in 1990, the schooner Madeline is a sail training and living history education vessel. *Address:* 13268 S. West Bayshore Dr *City:* Traverse City *State:* MI *Zip:* 49684 *Phone:* 231-946-2647 *Web:* www.maritimeheritagealliance.org *Email:* mark@maritimeheritagealliance.org *Visitors welcome?* Yes *Hours:* Contact attraction directly *Admission:* Contact attraction directly *Operated by:* Maritime Heritage Alliance *NR?* No *NHL?* No *Built:* 1990 *Latitude:* 45.3593 *Longitude:* -85.0713

MAGGIE LEE

The skipjack Maggie Lee is one of two remaining skipjacks with fore-and-aft planking. It is on exhibit at the Choptank River Heritage Center. *Address:* 10215 River Landing Rd. *City:* West Denton *State:* MI *Zip:* 21629 *Phone:* 410-479-4150 *Web:* choptankriverheritage.org *Email:* carolinemdhistory@gmail.com *Visitors welcome?* Yes *Hours:* May to September: Friday and Saturday, 11 a.m. to 3 p.m. *Admission:* Contact attraction directly *Operated by:* Choptank River Heritage Center *NR?* No *NHL?* No *Latitude:* 38.8881 *Longitude:* -75.8399

MAKANI OLU

Launched in 1998, the schooner Makani Olu (Gracious Wind) is a youth sailing training vessel. *Address:* 45-021 Likeke Pl. *City:* Kaneohe *State:* HI *Zip:* 96744 *Phone:* 808-349-3774 *Web:* www.marimed.org *Email:* info@marimed.org *Visitors welcome?* Yes *Hours:* Monday through Friday, 8 a.m. to 5 p.m. directly *Admission:* Contact attraction directly *Operated by:* Marimed Foundation *NR?* No *NHL?* No *Built:* 1998 *Latitude:* 21.4116 *Longitude:* -157.7780

MAMIE A. MISTER

Launched in 1911, the skipjack Mamie A. Mister is a working vessel on Chesapeake Bay. *City:* Deal Island *State:* MD *Visitors welcome?* No *Operated by:* Private owner *NR?* No *NHL?* No *Built:* 1911 *Latitude:* 38.1590 *Longitude:* -75.9480

MATTHEW TURNER

The 132-foot brigantine Matthew Turner is a sail education vessel. *Address:* #278, 3020 Bridgeway *City:* Sausalito *State:* CA *Zip:* 94965

Phone: 415-331-3214 *Web:* www.callofthesea.org *Email:* info@callofthesea.org *Visitors welcome?* Yes *Hours:* Contact attraction directly *Admission:* Contact attraction directly *Operated by:* Call of the Sea *NR?* No *NHL?* No *Built:* 2020 *Latitude:* 37.8704 *Longitude:* -122.5020

MANITOU

Launched in 1982, the schooner Manitou is an excursion vessel. *Address:* 13390 S.W. Bay Shore Dr. *City:* Traverse City *State:* MI *Zip:* 49684 *Phone:* 231-941-2000 *Web:* www.tallshipsailing.com *Email:* manitou@tallshipsailing.com *Visitors welcome?* Yes *Hours:* Contact attraction directly *Admission:* Contact attraction directly *Operated by:* Traverse Tall Ship Co. *NR?* No *NHL?* No *Built:* 1982 *Latitude:* 44.7840 *Longitude:* -85.6379

MARTHA (SCHOONER)

Launched in 1907, the schooner Martha is now an excursion and sail training vessel. *Address:* 380 Jefferson Street *City:* Port Townsend *State:* WA *Zip:* 98368 *Phone:* 206-310-8573 *Web:* www.schoonermartha.org *Email:* schoonermartha@yahoo.com *Visitors welcome?* Yes *Hours:* Contact attraction directly *Admission:* Contact attraction directly *Operated by:* Schooner Martha Foundation *NR?* Yes *NHL?* No *Built:* 1907 *Latitude:* 48.1184 *Longitude:* -122.7520

MARTHA LEWIS

Launched in 1955, the skipjack Martha Lewis is now an excursion and environmental education vessel. *Address:* 121 North Union Ave, Suite C *City:* Havre de Grace *State:* MD *Zip:* 21078 *Phone:* 410-939-4078 *Web:* www.skipjackmarthalewis.org *Email:* director@skipjackmarthalewis.org *Visitors welcome?* Yes *Hours:* Contact attraction directly *Admission:* Contact attraction directly *Operated by:* Chesapeake Heritage Conservancy *NR?* No *NHL?* No *Built:* 1955 *Latitude:* 39.5485 *Longitude:* -76.0911

MARY DAY

The schooner Mary Day is an excursion vessel. *Address:* Atlantic Ave. *City:* Camden *State:* ME *Zip:* 04843 *Phone:* 800-992-2218 *Web:* www.schoonermaryday.com` *Email:* info@maryday.com *Visitors welcome?* Yes *Hours:* Contact attraction directly *Admission:* Contact attraction directly *Operated by:* Schooner Mary Day *NR?* No *NHL?* No *Latitude:* 44.2098 *Longitude:* -69.0648

MARY E.

Launched in 1906, the schooner Mary E. is now an excursion vessel. *Address:* 243 Washington St. *City:* Bath Northport *State:* ME *Zip:* 04530 *Phone:* 207-443-1316 *Web:* www.mainemaritimemuseum.org *Email:* info@maritimeme.org *Visitors welcome?* Yes *Hours:* Contact attraction directly *Admission:* Contact attraction directly *Operated by:* Maine Maritime Museum *NR?* No *NHL?* No *Built:* 1906 *Latitude:* 43.8940 *Longitude:* -69.8159

MARY W. SOMERS

Launched in1904, the skipjack Mary W. Somers is a working vessel on Chesapeake Bay. *City:* St. Mary's City *State:* MD *Visitors welcome?* No *Operated by:* Private owner *NR?* No *NHL?* No *Built:* 1904 *Latitude:* 38.1871 *Longitude:* -76.4344

MARYLAND DOVE

The Maryland Dove is a re-creation of a 17th-century square-rigged vessel. The vessel is on display at Historic St. Mary's City. *Address:* 18751 Hogaboom Lane *City:* St. Mary's City *State:* MD *Zip:* 20686 *Phone:* 240-895-4990 Toll-free: 800-762-1634 *Web:* www.hsmcdigshistory.org *Email:* info@digshistory.org *Visitors welcome?* Yes *Hours:* Daily, 10 a.m. to 4 p.m. *Admission:* $10 adults, $9 seniors, $6 students w/ ID, Under five, FREE *Operated by:* Historic St. Mary's City *NR?* No *NHL?* No *Latitude:* 38.1724 *Longitude:* -76.4317

MAYFLOWER II

Mayflower II, the jewel of Plymouth Harbor, is a reproduction of the 17th-century ship that brought the English Colonists, (popularly known as Pilgrims) to Plymouth in 1620. Onboard visitors meet contemporary interpreters who speak about the reproduction. *Address:* State Pier, Plymouth Waterfront *City:* Plymouth *State:* MA *Zip:* 02360 *Phone:* 508-746-1622 *Web:* www.plimoth.org *Email:* info@plimoth.org *Visitors welcome?* Yes *Hours:* April - November:

daily, 9 a.m. to 5 p.m., with extended hours in summer months *Admission:* Contact attraction directly *Operated by:* Plimoth Plantation *NR?* No *NHL?* No *Built:* 1959 *Latitude:* 41.9584 *Longitude:* -70.6673

MERCANTILE

Launched in 1916, the schooner Mercantile is now an excursion vessel. *Address:* Camden Waterfront *City:* Camden *State:* ME *Zip:* 04843 *Phone:* 207-236-2938 Toll-free: 800-736-7981 *Web:* www.mainewindjammercruises.com *Email:* sail@mainewindjammercruises.com *Visitors welcome?* Yes *Hours:* Contact attraction directly *Admission:* Contact attraction directly *Operated by:* Maine Windjammer Cruises **NR? Yes NHL? Yes** *Built:* 1916 *Latitude:* 44.2098 *Longitude:* -69.0648

MIKE SEKUL

The Maritime & Seafood Industry Museum in Biloxi, Miss., has recaptured a piece of its history with their two schooners, the Glenn L. Swetman and the Mike Sekul. Available for day sailing or charter, the vessels can accommodate weddings, dockside partites, and other functions. *Address:* 115 First Street *City:* Biloxi *State:* MS *Zip:* 39530 *Phone:* 228-435-6320 *Web:* www.maritimemuseum.org *Email:* info@maritimemuseum.org *Visitors welcome?* Yes *Hours:* Monday through Saturday, 9 a.m. to 4:30 p.m.; Sunday, noon to 4 p.m. *Admission:* $10 adults; $8 seniors, active military; $6 students 5-15 *Operated by:* Maritime & Seafood Industry Museum *NR?* No *NHL?* No *Latitude:* 30.3937 *Longitude:* -88.8591

MINNIE V

Launched in 1906, the skipjack Minnie V. is now used as a floating classroom for at-risk youth programs. *Address:* 1417 Thames Street *City:* Baltimore *State:* MD *Zip:* 21231 *Phone:* 410-685-0295 *Web:* www.livingclassrooms.org *Visitors welcome?* Yes *Hours:* Contact attraction directly *Admission:* Contact attraction directly *Operated by:* Living Classrooms Foundation **NR? Yes** *NHL?* No *Built:* 1906 *Latitude:* 39.2864 *Longitude:* -76.6056

MISTRESS

Launched in 1967, the schooner Mistress is now an excursion vessel.

Address: Camden Waterfront *City:* Camden *State:* ME *Zip:* 04843
Phone: 207-236-2938 Toll-free: 800-736-7981 *Web:*
www.mainewindjammercruises.com *Email:*
sail@mainewindjammercruises.com *Visitors welcome?* Yes *Hours:*
Contact attraction directly *Admission:* Contact attraction directly
Operated by: Maine Windjammer Cruises *NR?* No *NHL?* No *Built:*
1967 *Latitude:* 44.2098 *Longitude:* -69.0648

MODESTY

Launched in 1923, the sloop Modesty is now an operational museum
vessel. *Address:* 86 West Ave. *City:* West Sayville *State:* NY *Zip:* 11796
Phone: 631-854-4974 *Web:* www.limaritime.org *Email:*
limm@limaritime.org *Visitors welcome?* Yes *Hours:* Monday to
Saturday: 10 a.m. to 4 p.m.; Sunday, noon to 4 p.m. *Admission:* $8
adults, $6 senior/child three to 17, under three FREE *Operated by:*
Long Island Maritime Museum *NR?* No *NHL?* No *Built:* 1923
Latitude: 40.7218 *Longitude:* -73.0938

MOSHULU

Launched in 1904, the barque Moshulu is now a floating restaurant.
Address: 401 S. Columbus Blvd. *City:* Philadelphia *State:* PA *Zip:* 19106
Phone: 215-923-2500 *Web:* www.moshulu.com *Email:*
info@moshulu.com *Visitors welcome?* Yes *Hours:* Contact attraction
directly *Admission:* Contact attraction directly *Operated by:* Moshulu
Restaurant *NR?* No *NHL?* No *Built:* 1904 *Latitude:* 39.9420 *Longitude:*
-75.1423

MYSTIC WHALER

Launched in 1967, the schooner Mystic Whaler is an excursion vessel.
Address: 35 Water St. *City:* New London *State:* CT *Zip:* 06320 *Phone:*
800-697-8420 *Web:* www.mysticwhaler.com *Email:*
info@mysticwhaler.com *Visitors welcome?* Yes *Hours:* Contact
attraction directly *Admission:* Contact attraction directly *Operated by:*
Mystic Whaler Cruises *NR?* No *NHL?* No *Built:* 1967 *Latitude:*
41.3569 *Longitude:* -72.0949

NATHAN OF DORCHESTER

Launched in 1992, the skipjack Nathan of Dorchester is an education vessel on Chesapeake Bay. *City:* Cambridge *State:* MD *Zip:* 21613 *Phone:* 410-228-7141 *Web:* www.skipjack-nathan.org *Email:* info@skipjack-nathan.org *Visitors welcome?* Yes *Hours:* Contact attraction directly *Admission:* Contact attraction directly *Operated by:* Dorchester Skipjack Committee *NR?* No *NHL?* No *Built:* 1992 *Latitude:* 38.5632 *Longitude:* -76.0788

OLIVER HAZARD PERRY

The full-rigged ship Oliver Hazard Perry is a sailing education vessel and the official tall ship of Rhode Island. The vessel is named for the US naval hero of the War of 1812. *Address:* 11a Bridge Street *City:* Newport *State:* RI *Zip:* 02840 Phone: 401-841-0080 Web: ohpri.org Email: info@ohpri.org *Visitors welcome?* Yes *Hours:* Contact attraction directly *Admission:* Contact attraction directly *Operated by:* Oliver Hazard Perry Rhode Island *NR?* No *NHL?* No *Built:* 2015 *Latitude:* 41.4922 *Longitude:* -71.3250

ONRUST

The yacht Onrust is a replica of a 1614 vessel believed to be the first ship built built in what is now New York State. *Address:* 67 Main Street *City:* Essex *State:* CT *Zip:* 06426 *Phone:* 860-767-8269 *Web:* ctrivermuseum.org/waterfront *Email:* crm@ctrivermuseum.org *Visitors welcome?* Yes *Hours:* Tuesday to Sunday, 10 a.m. to 5 p.m. *Admission:* $12 adults, $10 seniors, $9 students, $8 children six to 12, under six FREE *Operated by:* Connecticut River Museum *NR?* No *NHL?* No *Built:* 2009 *Latitude:* 41.3515 *Longitude:* -72.4209

LADONA

Launched in 1922, the schooner Ladona is an excursion vessel. *City:* Rockland *State:* ME *Zip:* 04841 *Phone:* 207-594-4723 Toll-free: 800-999-7352 *Web:* www.schoonerladona.com *Email:* info@schoonerladona.com *Visitors welcome?* Yes *Hours:* Contact attraction directly *Admission:* Contact attraction directly *Operated by:* Schooner Ladona *NR?* No *NHL?* No *Built:* 1922 *Latitude:* 44.1210 *Longitude:* -69.1239

NEITH

Launched in 1907, the cutter Neith is an excursion vessel. *City:* West

Mystic *State:* CT *Zip:* 06388 *Phone:* 860-460-5620 *Email:*
neith1907@sbcglobal.net *Visitors welcome?* Yes *Hours:* Contact
attraction directly *Admission:* Contact attraction directly *Operated by:*
Neith, LLC *NR?* No *NHL?* No *Built:* 1907 *Latitude:* 41.3544
Longitude: -71.9669

NELLIE L. BYRD

Launched in 1911, the skipjack Nellie L. Byrd is a working vessel on
Chesapeake Bay. *City:* Tilghman Island *State:* MD *Visitors welcome?* No
Operated by: Private owner **NR? Yes** *NHL?* No *Built:* 1911 *Latitude:*
38.7037 *Longitude:* -76.3386

NIAGARA

The Niagara is a reconstruction of the U.S. Navy warship that won
the Battle of Lake Erie in the war of 1812. The reconstruction
incorporates a small number of timbers recovered from the original
Niagara, which was scuttled in Lake Erie shortly after the War of
1812. *Address:* 150 East Front Street *City:* Erie *State:* PA *Zip:* 16507
Phone: 814-452-2744 *Web:* sailfnl.org *Email:* info@sailfnl.org *Visitors
welcome?* Yes *Hours:* Contact attraction directly *Admission:* Contact
attraction directly *Operated by:* Flagship Niagara League *NR?* No
NHL? No *Built:* 1998 *Latitude:* 42.1361 *Longitude:* -80.0837

NINA

Launched in 1992, the replica 15th-century caravel redondo Nina is
an operating museum vessel. *City:* St. Thomas *State:* VI *Zip:* 00803
Phone: 284-495-4618 *Web:* www.thenina.com *Email:*
columfnd@surfbvi.com *Visitors welcome?* Yes *Hours:* Contact
attraction directly *Admission:* Contact attraction directly *Operated by:*
Columbus Foundation *NR?* No *NHL?* No *Built:* 1992 *Latitude:*
18.3436 *Longitude:* -64.9314

OLAD

Launched in 1927, the schooner Olad is an excursion vessel. *City:*
Camden *State:* ME *Zip:* 04843 *Phone:* 207-236-2323 *Web:*
www.maineschooners.com *Email:* info@maineschooners.com *Visitors
welcome?* Yes *Hours:* Contact attraction directly *Admission:* Contact
attraction directly *Operated by:* Fully Found *NR?* No *NHL?* No *Built:*

1927 *Latitude:* 44.2098 *Longitude:* -69.0648

PEACEMAKER

Launched in 1989, the barkentine Peacemaker is a sail-training and excursion vessel. *City:* Brunswick *State:* GA *Phone:* 912-275-0001 *Web:* www.peacemakermarine.com *Email:* crew@peacemakermarine.com *Visitors welcome?* Yes *Hours:* Contact attraction directly *Admission:* Contact attraction directly *Operated by:* Peacemaker Marine *NR?* No *NHL?* No *Built:* 1989 *Latitude:* 31.1500 *Longitude:* -81.4915

PHILADELPHIA II

Philadelphia II is a modern replica of a Revolutionary War gunboat built to challenge the British Navy on Lake Champlain. The original Philadelphia sank in a 1776 naval engagement, and the remains were raised in 1935. The replica is used for living history education. *Address:* 4472 Basin Harbor Rd. *City:* Vergennes *State:* VT *Zip:* 05491 *Phone:* 802-475-2022 *Web:* www.lcmm.org *Email:* info@lcmm.org *Visitors welcome?* Yes *Hours:* Daily, 10 a.m. to 5 p.m. *Admission:* All ages, FREE *Operated by:* Lake Champlain Maritime Museum *NR?* No *NHL?* No *Built:* 1991 *Latitude:* 44.1973 *Longitude:* -73.3567

PIONEER

Launched in 1885, the schooner Pioneer is a floating exhibit at the South Street Seaport Museum. *Address:* 12 Fulton St. *City:* New York *State:* NY *Zip:* 10038 *Phone:* 212-748-8600 *Web:* www.southstreetseaportmuseum.org *Email:* info@southstseaport.org *Visitors welcome?* Yes *Hours:* Contact attraction directly *Admission:* Contact attraction directly *Operated by:* South Street Seaport Museum *NR?* No *NHL?* No *Built:* 1885 *Latitude:* 40.7066 *Longitude:* -74.0034

PIRATE

Launched in 1926, the Pirate is a Seattle-designed racing boat now on display at the Center for Wooden Boats. *Address:* Center For Wooden Boats, 1010 Valley Street *City:* Seattle *State:* WA *Phone:* 206-382-2628 *Web:* www.cwb.org *Email:* info@cwb.org *Visitors welcome?* Yes *Hours:* Contact attraction directly *Admission:* Contact attraction directly *Operated by:* Center for Wooden Boats **NR? Yes** *NHL?* No *Built:* 1926 *Latitude:* 47.6258 *Longitude:* -122.3370

PRIDE OF BALTIMORE II

Launched in 1988, the square-topsail schooner Pride of Baltimore II is a sail training vessel and goodwill ambassador for the city of Baltimore. *Address:* 401 East Pratt St. *City:* Baltimore *State:* MD *Zip:* 21202 *Phone:* 410-539-1151 *Web:* pride2.org *Email:* pride2@pride2.org *Visitors welcome?* Yes *Hours:* Contact attraction directly *Admission:* Contact attraction directly *Operated by:* Pride of Baltimore *NR?* No *NHL?* No *Built:* 1988 *Latitude:* 39.2859 *Longitude:* -76.6097

PRISCILLA

Launched in 1888, the schooner Priscilla is an operational museum vessel. *Address:* 88 West Ave. *City:* West Sayville *State:* NY *Zip:* 11796 *Phone:* 631-494-9888 *Web:* www.limaritime.org *Email:* limm@limaritime.org *Visitors welcome?* Yes *Hours:* Monday to Saturday: 10 a.m. to 4 p.m.; Sunday, noon to 4 p.m. *Admission:* $8 adults, $6 seniors and children *Operated by:* Long Island Maritime Museum *NR?* No *NHL?* No *Built:* 1888 *Latitude:* 40.7218 *Longitude:* -73.0938

Need help boarding? Most historic vessels and tall ships have limited ADA accessibility. However, crew are happy to assist if you call ahead to make arrangements.

PROVIDENCE

Launched in 1976, the sloop Providence is a living history and education vessel. *Address:* 1 Cameron St, Lower Level *City:* Alexandria *State:* VA *Zip:* 22314 *Phone:* 703-915-1600 *Web:* tallshipprovidence.org *Email:* info@tallshipprovidence.org *Visitors welcome?* Yes *Hours:* Contact attraction directly *Admission:* Contact attraction directly *Operated by:* Tall Ship Providence Foundation *NR?* No *NHL?* No *Built:* 1976 *Latitude:* 41.8211 *Longitude:* -71.4238

QUINNIPIACK

Launched in 1984, the schooner Quinnipiack is an environmental education vessel. *Address:* 60 South Water St. *City:* New Haven *State:* CT *Zip:* 06519 *Phone:* 203-865-1737 *Web:* www.schoonerinc.org *Email:* captain@schoonerinc.org *Visitors welcome?* Yes *Hours:* Contact attraction directly *Admission:* Contact attraction directly *Operated by:* Schooner, Inc *NR?* No *NHL?* No *Built:* 1984 *Latitude:* 41.2822 *Longitude:* -72.9285

R.H. LEDBETTER

The full-rigged ship R.H. Ledbetter is the flagship of the Culver Summer Naval School, located on Lake Maxinkuckee in Culver, Indiana. *Address:* 1300 Academy Rd. #138 *City:* Culver *State:* IN *Zip:* 46511 *Phone:* 574-842-8300 *Web:* www.culver.org/summer *Email:* summer@culver.org *Visitors welcome?* Yes *Hours:* Contact attraction directly *Admission:* Contact attraction directly *Operated by:* Culver Summer Schools & Camps *NR?* No *NHL?* No *Latitude:* 41.2224 *Longitude:* -86.4074

REBECCA T. RUARK

Launched in 1886, the skipjack Rebecca T. Ruark is now a working fishing and excursion vessel. *Address:* 21308 Phillips Road *City:* Tilghman *State:* MD *Zip:* 21671 *Phone:* 410-829-3976 *Web:* www.skipjack.org *Visitors welcome?* Yes *Hours:* Contact attraction directly *Admission:* Contact attraction directly *Operated by:* Capt. Wade H. Murphy, Jr. ***NR? Yes NHL? Yes*** *Built:* 1886 *Latitude:* 38.7095 *Longitude:* -76.3387

RED WITCH

Launched in 1986, the schooner Red Witch is an excursion and sail training vessel. *Address:* Kenosha Harbor South Seawall near 54th Street and 5th Avenue *City:* Kenosha *State:* WI *Zip:* 60611 *Web:* www.redwitch.com *Email:* RedWitchKenosha@gmail.com *Visitors welcome?* Yes *Hours:* Thursdays through Sundays *Admission:* Contact attraction directly *Operated by:* Lakeshore Sail Charters *NR?* No *NHL?* No *Built:* 1986 *Latitude:* 41.8910 *Longitude:* -87.6171

REGINA M

Launched in 1900, the fishing vessel Regina M. is part of the Mystic Seaport vessel collection. *Address:* 75 Greenmanville Avenue *City:* Mystic *State:* CT *Zip:* 06355 *Phone:* 860-572-5315 *Web:* www.mysticseaport.org *Visitors welcome?* Yes *Hours:* Thursday to Sunday, 10 a.m. to 4 p.m. *Admission:* $23.95 adults; $21.95 seniors;

$19.95 youth 13-17; $16.95 child 4-12 *Operated by:* Mystic Seaport: The Museum of America and the Sea *NR?* No *NHL?* No *Built:* 1900 *Latitude:* 41.3617 *Longitude:* -71.9634

RESOLUTE

Launched in 1939, the yawl Resolute is a sail training and education vessel. *City:* Steilacoom *State:* WA *Zip:* 98388 *Phone:* 253-588-3066 *Web:* www.resolutesailing.org *Email:* resolute@telisphere.com *Visitors welcome?* Yes *Hours:* Contact attraction directly *Admission:* Contact attraction directly *Operated by:* Resolute Sailing Foundation *NR?* No *NHL?* No *Built:* 1939 *Latitude:* 47.1698 *Longitude:* -122.6030

ROBERT C. SEAMANS

The brigantine Robert C. Seamans is a sail training and research vessel. *City:* Woods Hole *State:* MA *Zip:* 02543 *Phone:* 508-540-3954 Toll-free: 800-552-3633 *Web:* www.sea.edu *Email:* admission@sea.edu *Visitors welcome?* Yes *Hours:* Contact attraction directly *Admission:* Contact attraction directly *Operated by:* Sea Education Association *NR?* No *NHL?* No *Latitude:* 41.5302 *Longitude:* -70.6603

ROSEWAY

Launched in 1925, the schooner Roseway is a sail training and education vessel. *Address:* 9B Hospital St. *City:* Christiansted *State:* VI *Zip:* 00820 *Phone:* 340-626-7877 *Web:* www.worldoceanschool.org *Email:* info@worldoceanschool.org *Visitors welcome?* Yes *Hours:* Contact attraction directly *Admission:* Contact attraction directly *Operated by:* World Ocean School *NR?* No *NHL?* No *Built:* 1925 *Latitude:* 17.7488 *Longitude:* -64.7039

ROSIE PARKS

Designed specifically for dredging up the vast quantities of oysters found on the Chesapeake Bay's floor, Rosie Parks is one of a handful of skipjacks that continue to work the bay. *Address:* 213 N. Talbot Street *City:* St. Michaels *State:* MD *Zip:* 21663 *Phone:* 410-745-2916 *Web:* www.cbmm.org *Email:* cbland@cbmm.org *Visitors welcome?* Yes *Hours:* Daily, hours vary by season *Admission:* $16 adults; $13 seniors over 62, students; $12 retired military; $6 kids 6 to 17; active military, kids under 6 FREE *Operated by:* Chesapeake Bay Maritime Museum

NR? No *NHL?* No *Built:* 1955 *Latitude:* 38.7876 *Longitude:* -76.2249

SAN SALVADOR

Launched in 2015, San Salvador is a full-size replica of the ship sailed by Spanish explorer Juan Rodríguez Cabrillo to the west coast of North America in 1542. *Address:* 1492 North Harbor Drive *City:* San Diego *State:* CA *Zip:* 92101 *Phone:* 619-234-9153 *Web:* www.sdmaritime.com *Email:* info@sdmaritime.org *Visitors welcome?* Yes *Hours:* Daily, 10 a.m. to 8 p.m. *Admission:* $20 18+; $15 seniors, military, students; $10 children three to 12; children under two FREE *Operated by:* Maritime Museum Association of San Diego *NR?* No *NHL?* No *Built:* 1970 *Latitude:* 32.7276 *Longitude:* -117.1800

SANTA CLARA

The replica 15th-century caravel redondo Santa Clara is an operating museum ship. *City:* St. Thomas *State:* VI *Zip:* 00803 *Phone:* 284-495-4618 *Web:* www.thenina.com *Email:* columfnd@surfbvi.com *Visitors welcome?* Yes *Hours:* Contact attraction directly *Admission:* Contact attraction directly *Operated by:* Columbus Foundation *NR?* No *NHL?* No *Latitude:* 18.3436 *Longitude:* -64.9314

SEA GULL

Launched in 1924, the skipjack Sea Gull is a working vessel on Chesapeake Bay. *City:* Deal Island *State:* MD *Visitors welcome?* No *Operated by:* Private owner **NR? Yes** *NHL?* No *Built:* 1924 *Latitude:* 38.1590 *Longitude:* -75.9480

SEAWARD

Launched in 1988, the schooner Seaward is a sailing training and excursion vessel. *Address:* #278, 3020 Bridgeway *City:* Sausalito *State:* CA *Zip:* 94965 *Phone:* 415-331-3214 *Web:* www.callofthesea.org *Email:* info@callofthesea.org *Visitors welcome?* Yes *Hours:* Contact attraction directly *Admission:* Contact attraction directly *Operated by:* Call of the Sea *NR?* No *NHL?* No *Built:* 1988 *Latitude:* 37.8704 *Longitude:* -122.5020

SEMANA

Launched in 1975, the ketch Semana is a sail training and education vessel. *Address:* 5600 Royal Dane Mall, Suite 12 *City:* St. Thomas *State:* VI *Zip:* 00802 *Phone:* 207-321-9249 *Web:* www.sailingschool.com *Visitors welcome?* Yes *Hours:* Contact attraction directly *Admission:* Contact attraction directly *Operated by:* School of Ocean Sailing *NR?* No *NHL?* No *Built:* 1975 *Latitude:* 18.3436 *Longitude:* -64.9322

SHENANDOAH (SCHOONER)

Launched in 1964, the square topsail schooner Shenandoah is an excursion and sail training vessel. *City:* Vineyard Haven *State:* MA *Zip:* 02568 *Phone:* 508-693-1699 *Web:* theblackdogtallships.com *Email:* office@theblackdogtallships.com *Visitors welcome?* Yes *Hours:* Contact attraction directly *Admission:* Contact attraction directly *Operated by:* Black Dog Tall Ships *NR?* No *NHL?* No *Built:* 1964 *Latitude:* 41.4543 *Longitude:* -70.6036

SHERMAN ZWICKER

The Sherman Zwicker is a 142-foot wooden schooner built in 1942 in for the Zwicker and Co., by the Smith and Rhuland Shipyard in Lunenberg, Nova Scotia. The Sherman Zwicker is a transition vessel designed with a classic schooner hull. *Address:* Pier 25 *City:* New York *State:* NY *Phone:* 207-633-4727 *Web:* www.schoonermuseum.org *Email:* staff@schoonermuseum.org *Visitors welcome?* Yes *Hours:* Contact attraction directly *Admission:* Contact attraction directly *Operated by:* Maritime Foundation *NR?* No *NHL?* No *Built:* 1942 *Latitude:* 40.7203 *Longitude:* -74.0143

SIGSBEE

Launched in 1901, the skipjack Sigsbee is now used as a floating classroom for at-risk youth programs. *Address: Address:* 1417 Thames Street *City:* Baltimore *State:* MD *Zip:* 21231 *Phone:* 410-685-0295 *Web:* www.livingclassrooms.org *Visitors welcome?* Yes *Hours:* Contact attraction directly *Admission:* Contact attraction directly *Operated by:* Living Classrooms Foundation **NR? Yes** *NHL?* No *Built:* 1901 *Latitude:* 39.2864 *Longitude:* -76.6056

SOMERSET

Launched in 1949, the skipjack Somerset is a working vessel on Chesapeake Bay. *City:* Deal Island *State:* MD *Visitors welcome?* No

Operated by: Private owner *NR?* No *NHL?* No *Built:* 1949 *Latitude:* 38.1590 *Longitude:* -75.9480

SPIKE AFRICA

Launched in 1977, the schooner Spike Africa is an excursion vessel based in Friday Harbor, Wash. *Address:* 685 Spring Street *City:* Friday Harbor *State:* WA *Zip:* 98250 *Phone:* 360-378-2224 *Web:* www.sanjuansailcharter.com *Email:* info@schoonersnorth.com *Visitors welcome?* Yes *Hours:* Contact attraction directly *Admission:* Contact attraction directly *Operated by:* Spike Africa *NR?* No *NHL?* No *Built:* 1977 *Latitude:* 48.5313 *Longitude:* -123.0240

SPIRIT OF 1608

Launched in 2006, the John Smith barge Spirit of 1608 is a reproduction of a typical 17th-century barge used in the Chesapeake Bay area. It is an operating museum and excursion vessel. *Address:* 504 Main Street *City:* Reedville *State:* VA *Zip:* 22539 *Phone:* 804-453-6529 *Web:* www.rfmuseum.org *Visitors welcome?* Yes *Hours:* Thursday to Saturday, 11 a.m. to 4 p.m. *Admission:* $5 adults, $3 seniors, children 12 and under FREE *Operated by:* Reedville Fisherman's Museum *NR?* No *NHL?* No *Built:* 2006 *Latitude:* 37.8454 *Longitude:* -76.2742

SPIRIT OF DANA POINT

Launched in 1983, the schooner Spirit of Dana Point is a sail training and excursion vessel. *Address:* 24200 Dana Point Dr. *City:* Dana Point *State:* CA *Zip:* 92629 *Phone:* 949-496-2274 Toll-free: 949-496-4296 *Web:* www.oceaninstitute.org *Visitors welcome?* Yes *Hours:* Contact attraction directly *Admission:* Contact attraction directly *Operated by:* Ocean Institute *NR?* No *NHL?* No *Built:* 1983 *Latitude:* 33.4613 *Longitude:* -117.7070

On major holidays or summer weekends, demand for excursion tickets may be high. Call ahead or visit the ship's website to purchase tickets in advance.

SPIRIT OF MASSACHUSETTS

Launched in 1984, the schooner Spirit of Massachusetts is a floating restaurant. *Address:* 4 Western Ave. *City:* Kennebunkport *State:* ME *Zip:* 04043 *Web:* www.thespiritrestaurant.com *Email:* events@thespiritrestaurant.com *Visitors welcome?* Yes *Hours:* Contact attraction directly *Admission:* Contact attraction directly *Operated by:* The Spirit Restaurant *NR?* No *NHL?* No *Built:* 1984 *Latitude:* 43.3617 *Longitude:* -70.4769

SPIRIT OF SOUTH CAROLINA

Launched in 2007, the pilot schooner Spirit of South Carolina is a sail training and education vessel. *Address:* Charleston Maritime Center *City:* Charleston *State:* SC *Phone:* 843-696-0406 *Web:* spiritofsc.org *Email:* director@spiritofsc.com *Visitors welcome?* Yes *Hours:* Contact attraction directly *Admission:* Contact attraction directly *Operated by:* Spirit of South Carolina *NR?* No *NHL?* No *Built:* 2007 *Latitude:* 32.7766 *Longitude:* -79.9309

STANLEY NORMAN

Launched in 1902, the skipjack Stanley Norman is an educational vessel. *City:* Annapolis *State:* MD *Zip:* 21403 *Phone:* 888-728-3229 *Web:* www.cbf.org *Email:* chesapeake@cbf.org *Visitors welcome?* Yes *Hours:* Contact attraction directly *Admission:* Contact attraction directly *Operated by:* Chesapeake Bay Foundation *NR?* No *NHL?* No *Built:* 1902 *Latitude:* 38.9784 *Longitude:* -76.4922

STAR OF INDIA

Launched in 1863, the barque Star of India is a museum ship and the world's oldest active ship. She is owned and operated by the San Diego Maritime Museum. *Address:* 1492 North Harbor Drive *City:* San Diego *State:* CA *Zip:* 92101 *Phone:* 619-234-9153 *Web:* www.sdmaritime.com *Email:* info@sdmaritime.org *Visitors welcome?* Yes *Hours:* Daily, 10 a.m. to 8 p.m. *Admission:* $20 18+; $15 seniors, military, students; $10 children three to 12; children under two FREE *Operated by:* Maritime Museum Association of San Diego **NR? Yes NHL? Yes** *Built:* 1863 *Latitude:* 32.7276 *Longitude:* -117.1800

STEPHEN TABER

Launched in 1871, the schooner Stephen Taber is now an excursion vessel. *Address:* Windjammer Wharf *City:* Rockland *State:* ME *Zip:*

04841 *Phone:* 207-594-4723 Toll-free: 800-999-7352 *Web:* www.stephentaber.com *Email:* info@stephentaber.com *Visitors welcome?* Yes *Hours:* Contact attraction directly *Admission:* Contact attraction directly *Operated by:* Schooner Stephen Taber **NR? Yes NHL? Yes** *Built:* 1871 *Latitude:* 44.1037 *Longitude:* -69.1089

SULTANA

Launched in 2001, the schooner Sultana is a sail training and environmental education vessel. *Address:* 105 South Cross St. *City:* Chestertown *State:* MD *Zip:* 21620 *Phone:* 410-778-5954 *Web:* sultanaeducation.org *Email:* dmcmullen@sultanaprojects.org *Visitors welcome?* Yes *Hours:* Contact attraction directly *Admission:* Contact attraction directly *Operated by:* Sultana Projects *NR?* No *NHL?* No *Built:* 2001 *Latitude:* 39.2090 *Longitude:* -76.0665

SURPRISE (FULL-RIGGED SHIP)

Launched in 1970 as HMS Rose, HMS Surprise is a full rigged ship that appeared in the 2004 movie Master and Commander: The Far Side of the World. The vessel is now an excursion and museum ship for the San Diego Maritime Museum. *Address:* 1492 North Harbor Drive *City:* San Diego *State:* CA *Zip:* 92101 *Phone:* 619-234-9153 *Web:* www.sdmaritime.com *Email:* info@sdmaritime.org *Visitors welcome?* Yes *Hours:* Daily, 10 a.m. to 8 p.m. *Admission:* $20 18+; $15 seniors, military, students; $10 children three to 12; children under two FREE *Operated by:* Maritime Museum Association of San Diego *NR?* No *NHL?* No *Built:* 1970 *Latitude:* 32.7276 *Longitude:* -117.1800

SURPRISE (SCHOONER)

Launched in 1918, the schooner Surprise is now an excursion vessel. *Address:* Camden Harbor *City:* Camden *State:* ME *Zip:* 04843 *Phone:* 207-236-4687 *Web:* www.schoonersurprise.com *Email:* sail@schoonersurprise.com *Visitors welcome?* Yes *Hours:* Contact attraction directly *Admission:* Contact attraction directly *Operated by:* Schooner Surprise **NR? Yes** *NHL?* No *Built:* 1918 *Latitude:* 44.2143 *Longitude:* -69.0580

SUSAN CONSTANT

Launched in 1991, the Susan Constant is a working replica of a ship that brought the first colonists to the Jamestown settlement in 1607. *Address:* 2218 Jamestown Rd. *City:* Williamsburg *State:* VA *Zip:* 23185 *Phone:* 757-253-7308 *Web:* historyisfun.org *Visitors welcome?* Yes *Hours:* Daily, 10 a.m. to 4:30 p.m *Admission:* Contact attraction directly *Operated by:* Jamestown-Yorktown Foundation *NR?* No *NHL?* No *Built:* 1991 *Latitude:* 37.2251 *Longitude:* -76.7862

SUSAN MAY

Launched in 1901, the skipjack Susan May is a working vessel on Chesapeake Bay. *City:* Wenona *State:* MD *Visitors welcome?* No *Operated by:* Private owner ***NR? Yes*** NHL? No *Built:* 1901 *Latitude:* 38.1390 *Longitude:* -75.9502

SWIFT OF IPSWICH

Built in 1938 as a replica of a 1787 schooner, the Swift of Ipswich was the private yacht of actor James Cagney for a number of years. A fast schooner, the Swift has served southern California youth since joining the LAMI fleet in 1991. *Address:* Berth 84, Foot of 6th St. *City:* San Pedro *State:* CA *Zip:* 90731 *Phone:* 310-833-6055 *Web:* www.lamitopsail.org *Email:* info@lamitopsail.org *Visitors welcome?* Yes *Hours:* Contact attraction directly *Admission:* Contact attraction directly *Operated by:* Los Angeles Maritime Institute *NR?* No *NHL?* No *Built:* 1938 *Latitude:* 33.7387 *Longitude:* -118.2790

SYLVINA W. BEAL

Launched in 1911, the Sylvina W. Beal is undergoing restoration. *City:* Essex *State:* ME *Phone:* 978-290-7168 *Web:* schooneradelle.com *Email:* info@schoonerardelle.com Visitors welcome: Yes *Hours:* Contact attraction directly *Admission:* Contact attraction directly Operated by Schooner Ardelle *NR?* No NHL: No *Built:* 1911 *Latitude:* 42.6320 *Longitude:* -70.7829

TABOR BOY

Launched in 1914, the schooner Tabor Boy is now an education vessel at Tabor Academy. *Address:* 66 Spring Street *City:* Marion *State:* MA *Zip:* 2738 *Phone:* 508-748-2000 *Web:* www.taboracademy.org *Email:* info@taboracademy.org *Visitors welcome?* Yes *Hours:* Contact attraction directly *Admission:* Contact attraction directly *Operated by:*

Tabor Academy *NR?* No *NHL?* No *Built:* 1914 *Latitude:* 41.7067 *Longitude:* -70.7682

TALBOT LADY

Launched in 1986, the skipjack Talbot Lady is a working vessel on Chesapeake Bay. *City:* Canton *State:* NJ *Visitors welcome?* No *Operated by:* Private owner *NR?* No *NHL?* No *Built:* 1986 *Latitude:* 39.4709 *Longitude:* -75.4149

THOMAS E. LANNON

The schooner Thomas E. Lannon offers two-hour sails from Seven Seas Wharf at the Gloucester House Restaurant, Rogers Street, Gloucester from mid-May through the end of October. *Address:* 63 Rogers St. *City:* Gloucester *State:* MA *Zip:* 01930 *Phone:* 978-281-6634 *Web:* www.schooner.org *Email:* info@schooner.org *Visitors welcome?* Yes *Hours:* Contact attraction directly *Admission:* Contact attraction directly *Operated by:* Schooner Thomas E. Lannon *NR?* No *NHL?* No *Built:* 1997 *Latitude:* 41.7001 *Longitude:* -71.4162

THOMAS W. CLYDE

Launched in 1911, the skipjack Thomas W. Clyde is a working vessel on Chesapeake Bay. *City:* Tilghman Island *State:* MD *Visitors welcome?* No *Operated by:* Private owner **NR?** **Yes** *NHL?* No *Built:* 1911 *Latitude:* 38.7037 *Longitude:* -76.3386

TREE OF LIFE

Launched in 1991, the schooner Tree of Life is a sail training and excursion vessel. *Address:* 100 Metro Center Blvd. *City:* Warwick *State:* RI *Zip:* 02886 *Phone:* 401-474-7150 *Web:* www.schoonertreeoflife.com *Email:* captainmorse@schoonertreeoflife.com *Visitors welcome?* Yes *Hours:* Contact attraction directly *Admission:* Contact attraction directly *Operated by:* Schooner Tree of Life *NR?* No *NHL?* No *Built:* 1991 *Latitude:* 41.4736 *Longitude:* -71.3086

UTOPIA

The schooner Utopia is a sail training and education vessel. *Address:* 100 Dame St. *City:* Suttons Bay *State:* MI *Zip:* 49682 *Phone:* 231-271-

3077 *Web:* www.schoolship.org *Email:* isea@schoolship.org *Visitors welcome?* Yes *Hours:* Monday through Friday, 8:30 a.m. to 5 p.m. *Admission:* Contact attraction directly *Operated by:* Inland Seas Education Association *NR?* No *NHL?* No *Built:* 1994 *Latitude:* 44.9750 *Longitude:* -85.6497

VENTURA

Launched in 1922, the centerboard cutter Ventura is now an excursion vessel. *Address:* World Financial Center, North Cove Marina *City:* New York *State:* NY *Zip:* 10274 *Phone:* 929-379-7967 *Web:* sailnewyork.com *Email:* ventura@sailnewyork.com *Visitors welcome?* Yes *Hours:* Contact attraction directly *Admission:* Contact attraction directly *Operated by:* S/V Ventura *NR?* No *NHL?* No *Built:* 1922 *Latitude:* 40.7131 *Longitude:* -74.0286

VICTORY CHIMES

Launched in 1900, the three-masted ram schooner Victory Chimes is now an excursion vessel. *Address:* Foot of Tillson Avenue *City:* Rockland *State:* ME *Phone:* 800-745-5651 *Web:* www.victorychimes.com *Email:* info@victorychimes.com *Visitors welcome?* Yes *Hours:* Contact attraction directly *Admission:* Contact attraction directly *Operated by:* Victory Chimes **NR? Yes NHL? Yes** *Built:* 1900 *Latitude:* 44.1044 *Longitude:* -69.1054

VIRGINIA

Launched in 2004, the schooner Virginia is a recreation of a typical Chesapeake Bay pilot schooner. It operates as a sail training and living history education vessel. *Address:* One Waterside Drive *City:* Norfolk *State:* VA *Zip:* 23510 *Phone:* 757-664-1000 *Web:* www.schoonervirginia.org *Visitors welcome?* Yes *Hours:* Contact attraction directly *Admission:* Contact attraction directly *Operated by:* Nauticus *NR?* No *NHL?* No *Built:* 2004 *Latitude:* 36.8458 *Longitude:* -76.2883

VIRGINIA W

Launched in 1904, the skipjack Virginia W. is a working vessel on Chesapeake Bay. *City:* Kinsale *State:* VA *Visitors welcome?* No *Operated by:* Private owner **NR? Yes** *NHL?* No *Built:* 1904 *Latitude:* 38.0296

Longitude: -76.5808

WAVERTREE

Launched in 1885, the ship Wavertree is now a floating exhibit. *Address:* 12 Fulton St. *City:* New York *State:* NY *Zip:* 10038 *Phone:* 212-748-8600 *Web:* www.southstreetseaportmuseum.org *Email:* info@southstseaport.org *Visitors welcome?* Yes *Hours:* Contact attraction directly *Admission:* Contact attraction directly *Operated by:* South Street Seaport Museum *NR? Yes* NHL? No *Built:* 1885 *Latitude:* 40.7066 *Longitude:* -74.0034

WELCOME (SLOOP)

Launched in 1976 and rebuilt in 2007, the armed sloop replica Welcome is a sailing training and living history education vessel on the Great Lakes. *Address:* 13268 S. West Bayshore Dr *City:* Traverse City *State:* MI *Zip:* 49684 *Phone:* 231-946-2647 *Web:* www.maritimeheritagealliance.org *Email:* mark@maritimeheritagealliance.org *Visitors welcome?* Yes *Hours:* Contact attraction directly *Admission:* Contact attraction directly *Operated by:* Maritime Heritage Alliance NR? No NHL? No *Built:* 1976 *Latitude:* 45.3593 *Longitude:* -85.0713

WENDAMEEN

Launched in 1912, the gaff-rigged schooner yacht Wendameen is now an excursion vessel. *Address:* Maine State Pier, 56 Commercial St. *City:* Portland *State:* ME *Zip:* 04101 *Phone:* 207-766-2500 Toll-free: 877-246-6637 *Web:* www.portlandschooner.com *Email:* sails@portlandschooner.com *Visitors welcome?* Yes *Hours:* Contact attraction directly *Admission:* Contact attraction directly *Operated by:* Portland Schooner Company *NR? Yes* NHL? No *Built:* 1912 *Latitude:* 43.6577 *Longitude:* -70.2500

WILMA LEE

Launched in 1940, the skipjack Wilma Lee is a working vessel on Chesapeake Bay. *City:* Kinsale *State:* VA *Visitors welcome?* No *Operated by:* Private owner *NR? Yes* NHL? No *Built:* 1940 *Latitude:* 38.0296 *Longitude:* -76.5808

WINDY

Launched in 1996, the schooner Windy is a sail training and excursion vessel. *Address:* 600 E. Gand Ave., Navy Pier *City:* Chicago *State:* IL *Zip:* 60611 *Phone:* 312-451-2700 *Web:* www.tallshipwindy.com *Email:* tickets@tallshipwindy.com *Visitors welcome?* Yes *Hours:* Contact attraction directly *Admission:* Contact attraction directly *Operated by:* Tall Ship Windy *NR?* No *NHL?* No *Built:* 1996 *Latitude:* 41.8919 *Longitude:* -87.6041

WOODWIND

Launched in 1993, the schooner Woodwind and her sister Woodwind II are sail training and excursion vessel. *Address:* 80 Compromise St. *City:* Annapolis *State:* MD *Zip:* 21401 *Phone:* 410-263-7837 *Web:* www.schoonerwoodwind.com *Email:* info@schoonerwoodwind.com *Visitors welcome?* Yes *Hours:* Contact attraction directly *Admission:* Contact attraction directly *Operated by:* Running Free *NR?* No *NHL?* No *Built:* 1993 *Latitude:* 38.9756 *Longitude:* -76.4859

WOODWIND II

Launched in 1993, the schooner Woodwind and her sister Woodwind II are sail training and excursion vessels. *Address:* 80 Compromise St. *City:* Annapolis *State:* MD *Zip:* 21401 *Phone:* 410-263-7837 *Web:* www.schoonerwoodwind.com *Email:* info@schoonerwoodwind.com *Visitors welcome?* Yes *Hours:* Contact attraction directly *Admission:* Contact attraction directly *Operated by:* Running Free *NR?* No *NHL?* No *Built:* 1993 *Latitude:* 38.9756 *Longitude:* -76.4859

YANKEE CLIPPER

Launched in 1941, the ketch Yankee Clipper is a sail training vessel that works with the Sea Scouts. *Address:* Fisherman's Terminal *City:* Seattle *State:* WA *Web:* seascoutshipyankeeclipper.com *Email:* stevengrassia@gmail.com *Visitors welcome?* Yes *Hours:* Contact attraction directly *Admission:* Contact attraction directly *Operated by:* Yankee Clipper Foundation *NR?* No *NHL?* No *Built:* 1941 *Latitude:* 47.6062 *Longitude:* -122.3320

ZODIAC

Launched in 1924, the schooner Zodiac is now an excursion vessel.

City: Bellingham *State:* WA *Phone:* 206-719-7622 *Web:* www.schoonerzodiac.com *Visitors welcome?* Yes *Hours:* Contact attraction directly *Admission:* Contact attraction directly *Operated by:* Vessel Zodiac Corporation **NR? Yes** *NHL?* No *Built:* 1924 *Latitude:* 48.7519 *Longitude:* -122.4787

PRESSED FOR TIME? FYDDEYE RECOMMENDS	
Alma	Part of large ship collection
Lady Washington	Pirates of the Caribbean movie
Pride of Baltimore II	Replica privateer vessel
Wavertree	Larger than most tall ships

INDEX OF SHIPS

ABOUT THE AUTHOR

Joe Follansbee is the author of five maritime history books, including *Shipbuilders, Sea Captains and Fishermen: The Story of the Schooner Wawona*, *Blowing Out the Stink: Life on a Lumber and Cod Schooner, 1897-1947*, *The Fyddeye Guide to America's Maritime History*, *The Fyddeye Guide to America's Lighthouses*, *The Fyddeye Guide to America's Veteran Warships*, *The Fyddeye Guide to America's Maritime Museums*. He has written a novel for young adults based on his maritime research, *Bet: Stowaway Daughter*. As J.G. Follansbee, he's written six science fiction and fantasy novels. He lives in Seattle.

BOOKS BY JOE FOLLANSBEE

Maritime History and Culture

- *Shipbuilders, Sea Captains, and Fishermen: The Story of the Schooner Wawona*
- *Blowing Out the Stink: Life on a Lumber and Cod Schooner, 1897-1947*
- The Fyddeye Guides
  - *The Fyddeye Guide to America's Maritime History*
  - *The Fyddeye Guide to America's Lighthouses*
  - *The Fyddeye Guide to America's Veteran Warships*
  - *The Fyddeye Guide to America's Maritime Museums*
- *Bet: Stowaway Daughter* (young adult fiction)

Science Fiction and Fantasy (writing as J.G. Follansbee)

- Tales From a Warming Planet
  - *The Mother Earth Insurgency*
  - *Carbon Run*
  - *City of Ice and Dreams*
  - *Restoration*
- The Future History of the Grail
  - *Fall of the Green Land*
  - *War for the Green Land*
  - *Return to the Green Land*

Made in the USA
Columbia, SC
10 September 2021